THE WINTER MEN

The Seventh All Blacks Tour

THE WINTER MEN

The Seventh All Blacks Tour

Now is the winter of our discontent . . .
— *Richard III*

Wallace Reyburn

STANLEY PAUL/LONDON

STANLEY PAUL & CO LTD

3 Fitzroy Sq., London W1

AN IMPRINT OF THE HUTCHINSON GROUP

London Melbourne Sydney Auckland
Wellington Johannesburg Cape Town
and agencies throughout the world.

First published 1973

This book has been set in Baskerville, printed in Great Britain by
The Stellar Press Welham Green, Hatfield, Hertfordshire
and bound by Leighton-Straker
Bookbinders of London.

ISBN 0 09 116350 1

CONTENTS

ACKNOWLEDGEMENTS

The author acknowledges the following for permission to reproduce illustrations of which they own the copyright:

Mike Brett, Chris Smith, Colorsport, Press Association

ILLUSTRATIONS

PART ONE

The Tour

I

End of Long Era?

ONE is tempted to say that this is the end of an era—a long era stretching right back to August 13, 1904.

It was on that day, in Wellington, that the British and New Zealand played their first ever Test—and the British side was convincingly beaten, 9–3. 'Start as you intend to go on' was unfortunately true. The British were to go on being beaten in New Zealand for decade after decade, never able to win a Test series, recording only two isolated victories in individual matches, one in 1930 and another in 1959.

And it was the same the other way around. New Zealand sent her All Blacks over here and they rode roughshod over practically everything the British Isles had to offer. In six tours extending over more than sixty years they lost merely seven of the 157 matches they played.

If ever the term 'near invincibility' could be accurately used it most certainly applied to the All Blacks as far as the British were concerned.

And then, lo and behold, the British Lions in New Zealand in 1971 took it upon themselves to ride roughshod over every provincial side put up against them and to win for the first time ever a Test series there.

Was this a turning point? The visit of the Seventh All Blacks to Britain in the 1973–4 season would give the answer. And what happened? British teams inflicted on them the worst record of any New Zealand side to tour the British Isles. The latest version of the Near Invincibles lost more matches than on the three previous tours combined! And clonk they went to the bottom of the league table of New Zealand teams in Britain:

	Played	Won	Lost	Drawn
1924–5	28	28	–	–
1967–8	11	10	–	1
1905–6	32	31	1	–
1963–4	30	28	1	1
1953–4	28	24	2	2
1935–6	28	24	3	1
1973–4	**26**	**20**	**4**	**2**

It would seem on the face of it that the All Blacks' long era of one-sided domination over Britain has been brought to an end. And the explanation for it would be simple. In all those previous decades New Zealand had the unfair advantage that theirs were *coached* teams, bred of competitive rugby, playing against players without such 'semi-pro' preparation, who in the main had the 'I'm only here for the beer' attitude to their weekend outings at their club—the jolly runaround on the rugger field merely being a prelude to getting pissed in the pavilion. Then as the 1960s drew to a close the new generation of British rugby players let it be known that they were tired of their country being perpetual good losers to the All Blacks. They insisted that the game be approached with the same dedication of the New Zealanders. And the results were immediate. Meeting the All Blacks now on something like equal terms, they have cut them down to size.

But it isn't as simple as that, when you look into it more closely.

Although from a Britisher's point of view it would be wonderful to be able to say that that the Seventh All Blacks suffered simply because of the great improvement in British rugby, it doesn't really hold water.

What the British did to these All Blacks was only fractionally better than in 1935–6. And it could be argued that they didn't do as well. Both Wales and England beat the 1935 side. Yet none of the Home Countries succeeded in beating the All Blacks in an International this time, despite the supposed benefits of coaching, assiduous midweek training and the other forms of dedication unknown in Britain in the 1930s.

The plain fact of the matter is that in 1935–6 the British

caught the New Zealanders when their rugby was at a low ebb, when they had been forced to abandon their highly successful 2–3–2 scrum and conform to the 8-man scrum and had not yet learned to cope with this radical difference.

Again on this new tour the British caught the All Blacks when they were below par, due to the retirement *en masse* of Meads & Co. Some might say that this, rather than improved British rugby, was the root of those four defeats and two draws.

It was undoubtedly a young, inexperienced side. I can't remember such a 'Who's he?' team when I watched their first practice at Richmond just after they arrived. The assembled rugby writers, thumbing through the publicity handout, found that a third of the side were listed as 'a new All Black', let alone having Test experience. The whole 30 players averaged only three caps per head—compared to 17 per man in the team they were to meet in the first Test against Wales, and against Ireland—just short of a staggering average of 20 Test appearances per man. Innocents abroad, that was what the Seventh All Blacks were as far as big-time rugby was concerned.

At the conclusion of this initial leg-stretcher at Richmond (characterised by a lot of energetic running about by a little fellow who was apparently named Batty), a reporter asked coach Bob Duff what sort of training session he felt they had had. 'I wouldn't call that a training session,' he said. Sad to relate, that was what more than a few observers were to comment about many a fully-fledged practice Duff was to conduct as the tour got under way.

Bob Duff will not be numbered among the great All Black coaches. A forward in his playing days (11 caps in the 1950s), his heart was in the pack, although he invited us to believe it was elsewhere. When the British public were pleasantly surprised at the sparkling display of 15-man rugby in the All Blacks' opening game against Western Counties, Duff said: 'This was a most satisfying start to the tour. We have no intention of playing 10-man rugby. I have no idea where people in Britain got the idea from, as in my view New Zealand have never played in this way.' Either he thought that the British were so naive as to swallow this or else he had a bad lapse of memory. Duff made his All Black debut touring Australia in 1951 with fly-half Laurie Haig, one of the most notorious exponents of 10-man rugby New Zealand has ever produced, as rugby fans here knew to their sorrow when Haig was the man most responsible for making the 1953-4 tour of Britain such a drab affair.

Duff knew about 10-man rugby all right, as became evident later in the tour. His knowledge of backplay was sketchy and this meant that in his training sessions that sphere was left very much in the hands of Sid Going, an odd place to put it in view of Going's known inclination not merely towards the 10-man game but to something even worse—9-man rugby.

The veterans among the New Zealand correspondents with the team were not enthusiastic about the Duff practices, having seen men such as Fred Allen in coaching action. Bored with watching the repeated run-and-ruck drilling of the forwards—'Drop the ball. . . . Drive over it. . . . Drive! Drive! Drive!'—they wondered just how bored the forwards themselves were with the lack of variety in their diet.

Duff announced that he was cooking up 'secret moves' with which his team would confound their opponents. The correspondents, tongue in cheek, whispered that one surprise item he had evolved was to get the full-back to come up and join the three-quarter line in attack . . . and they could hardly believe their ears when in fact they heard Duff discussing with Karam this novel ploy.

So—this young side, coached without distinction, was there for the taking. Carwyn James at Llanelli helped himself. In the North West of England and in the West Midlands they did likewise. And in the last match of the British part of the tour the Barbarians, playing brilliant British Lions rugby, had a field day.

But why did not the thoroughly coached, painstakingly prepared teams of the four Home Countries do the same in the Internationals? It would seem that the 'improved British rugby' has not improved enough. This definitely not great All Black side was allowed to keep intact New Zealand's unbeaten record in Internationals in the British Isles which is now of 20 years' standing.

It was illuminating to watch the Ireland-England match in

Dublin just after the All Blacks quitted these islands. Main characteristic of this bad sample of rugby was the Collapsed Ruck, which for so long had been a feature of Home Internationals. This match seemed to put British rugby right back where it started before intensified coaching had been introduced. Here again was the old, old story: player runs with ball, is tackled, other players of both sides assemble at the point of breakdown, they all collapse in a heap, referee blows for a scrum. We had fondly thought that, taking the slick rucking of Whineray's men and Lochore's as a model, the British had brought that all to an end in their own rugby.

But no. Still breakaway forwards (and backs) seem quite unable to learn the simple lesson that you don't go into what is going to develop into a ruck with the ball in front of you—you have it down at one side or you back into the tackle, so that it can be made available quickly and cleanly for your backs to be on the move.

Bob Duff may have been an unimaginative coach, but it must be said for him that in his obsession with rucking he was at least backing the right horse. It had been the basis of the success of his team's predecessors and it was something the British could just not get the hang of—for example, the wasted breaks of Ripley and Neary in the England Test. In the All Black philosophy 'possession is all'. The Home Countries each had something like parity in possession from set pieces—better at scrummaging, not all that unsuccessful at the line-out—but when it came to rucking always the All Blacks outclassed them. And surely it is self-evident that quick possession from a ruck, when the defence is at sixes and sevens, is far more advantageous than at a set piece, when the defence is all lined up ready.

When Britain's rugbymen manage to get this message, then the All Blacks will not only partially but fully be cut down to size.

PUB DIRECTIONS

In the days of the Mighty Pinetree the story that went the rounds to intimidate British opponents was that before each major fixture the All Blacks undertook in New Zealand a posse used to go out and lasso Meads and bring him down from the hills. The intimidation story which accompanied these new All Blacks over here was that when the selectors are choosing their forwards they go out in to the country and talk to the farmers ploughing their fields. Each is asked: 'Where's the nearest pub?' If they point with their hands they're not considered for selection. But if they point with the plough—!

KIRKPATRICK'S EUROPE XV

Of all the rugby talent in Britain and France that the All Blacks encountered during their tour, who most impressed them? A good guide to this is provided by the Europe XV picked by Ian Kirkpatrick for the French sports daily *L'Equipe*:

Full-back: John Williams (Wales) or Irvine (Scotland)
Wings: Duckham (England) and Davies (Wales) or Steele (Scotland)
Centres: Gibson (Ireland) and
Fly-half: McGann (Ireland)
Scrum-half: Barrau (France)
No. 8: Ripley (England) or Spanghero (France)
Flankers: Tom David (Wales) and Slattery (Ireland) or MacEwan (Scotland)
Locks: Ralston (England) and Bastiat (France)
Props: Llewelyn (Wales) and McLoughlin (Ireland) or Lynch (Ireland) or Carmichael (Scotland)
Hooker: Pullin (England) or Kennedy (Ireland)

David is the only uncapped player but everybody else along with Kirkpatrick knew that it would be only a matter of time before the Welsh selectors remedied that. His choice of Bastiat as one of the locks is interesting, since the French did not think he was good enough to face the All Blacks in the Test. He made a great impression on the New Zealanders in the Tarbes match. As to the spare place for a centre, one feels sure that if Kirkpatrick had thought a little harder the name of Dawes would have come to mind. Captain of the triumphant 1971 Lions and of the equally triumphant Barbarians against Kirkpatrick's team . . . but perhaps, since Dawes had retired from International rugby, he wasn't regarded as available for this imaginary side.

NEGATIVE APPROACH

It might have been thought as this was a team reputed to be colourless (the 'All Greys') and in certain respects an unpopular side, it would not have had the same pulling power of such crowd-pleasers as the teams of Whineray in 1963 and Lochore in 1967. Not a bit of it. They pulled in 780,000 cash customers on the tour, which compares with the 750,000 who turned out in New Zealand to watch the glamorous 1971 Lions, even allowing for the fact that there were fewer matches on that tour.

Why did the crowds roll up to watch these All Blacks, almost without exception taxing the capacity of every ground at which they played? The explanation is simple. A team ripe for the plucking (Llanelli had proved that as early as the second match), the crowds rolled up in the hopeful expectation of seeing them beaten.

2
Management and Morale

WHEN the All Blacks trotted out on to the field for their first match at Gloucester the crowd sensed that something was wrong, but couldn't quite put their finger on it. Then as the team lined up for the kick-off they realised what it was—the All Blacks were not going to do a haka! A buzz of disappointment went around the ground. Perhaps they hadn't had time to rehearse it. Probably they'd get going with it in the next match or so. But they didn't. The shattering news was announced that these All Blacks had abandoned the haka.

A trivial matter? Not at all. The haka was a tradition, going back over more than half a century, part of the All Black image, the little touch that put them colourfully apart from other touring sides. Manager Ernie Todd said that abandoning the haka had been a decision of the players. What had it got to do with them? What right had they to dispense with this import-ant component of 'the magic of the All Blacks'? It was akin to Welsh players of today saying 'Let's ditch *Land of Our Fathers*'.

Already suspected of being a team without personality, the scrapping of the haka tended to confirm this and contributed in no small measure to the tour getting off on the wrong foot as far as public acceptance and team morale were concerned.

In their final match in Britain, against the Barbarians, they did commence proceedings with a haka—and got what sounded like the biggest round of applause of their tour. But by then it was a bit late to start mending their fences, to try to undo the damage they had done in numerous respects to the All Black image.

A New Zealander by birth, I had always in the past done some national gloating whenever the All Blacks were mentioned. When rugbymen here talked of touring teams they dismissed the Wallabies as Aussie roughnecks. The Springboks—well, we know what the feeling about them is. But the All Blacks—ah, that was different. I always felt a glow of pride when Britishers talked about the All Blacks. They were popular. Now, however, we had this new contingent and from the outset they seemed determined in a single tour to wreck the good name their predecessors had built up over a period of 60 years.

The 1935 All Black tour was the first rugby tour I covered so I have first-hand knowledge of only five of the seven New Zealand touring teams here, but I do think it is safe to say that these seemed to be of a different breed from those who had come before. I was not alone in this. Midway through the tour the *New Zealand Herald* said: 'A certain arrogance of mind in some players and a tendency towards churlishness and indiscipline have been noticeable.'

Manager Todd made no mention of this and similar comments in their own Press when he stated at every opportunity, right up to his parting shot as the team left for home, that the British Press had conducted a smear campaign against them. Captain Ian Kirkpatrick joined him in these accusations, which did not help his personal image. If there had been a so-called smear campaign against this side, why wasn't there one also against the 1967 All Blacks? Kirkpatrick was on that tour and knew very well there wasn't. Just as there wasn't against Whineray's 1963 side, or other previous All Blacks. As we have said, the New Zealanders have always been popular visitors. Why should the Press suddenly decide to knock this particular side with what Todd termed 'unfounded statements'? The fact of the matter was that they just reported accurately the 'arrogance, churlishness and indiscipline'.

As to arrogance. . . . At the first social function—the New Zealand High Commissioner's big party for the team, British rugby officials and others—people watching Kirkpatrick trying to round up the players at time of leaving sensed there could be trouble ahead for the management. There is an old-fashioned word, 'sassy', used of children being rude to their parents, others towards those in authority. It was applicable to more than a few of this side.

As the tour got under way, watching their rudeness, hearing

their public swearing, it was interesting to try to figure out what was behind this change from the All Blacks who had come before.

Always any visiting New Zealanders and Australians, not only rugby players, have suffered from an inferiority complex when confronted with the more sophisticated, more wordly way of life here. Not surprising when they've been made aware that 'the only culture New Zealand has is agriculture' and that 'Australians must be wonderful people because, after all, they were chosen by the best English Judges'. And they coped with this feeling of inferiority in different ways. The Australians, out to let it be known that they were building a nation of their own, tended to bash their way through, tended to be belligerent. On the other hand the New Zealander, content to have his country regarded as a little bit of old England transplanted out to the South Pacific, tended to retire into his shell. The two basic ways to counter an inferiority complex.

But now a sector of the young players in this team who were to influence the others showed clearly that theirs was not the customary New Zealand approach. One wondered why? Was it nothing more nor less than an outgrowth of the general Revolt of Youth, of which so much has been seen and heard in the older world and now taken up by New Zealanders? Was it a reflection of a changed attitude towards 'dear old England', who of late had been doing unfriendly things like the Common Market and slapping immigration restrictions on New Zealanders who formerly had been able to enter the country freely? Or was it that they felt it was about time New Zealand came of age and, like Australians, they'd make their presence felt? Whatever the root cause, they seemed to be serving notice that they weren't going to be the well behaved visitors their forerunners had been.

As to what the *New Zealand Herald* called their churlishness. . . . An explanation of why they earned that early reputation of being a sullen crew might have been that they were beaten in their second match, a disaster for a country that takes its rugby so seriously. But Whineray's 1963 team lost their third match and it had no similar effect on them.

However, what was definitely a contributing factor to low

team morale was that they had a 'bussing' problem like the
Americans, although of a different type. This tour differed
from previous ones in that in their incessant travels up, down
and across the country fulfilling their fixtures they went far
more by coach than by train, as in the other tours. Constantly
they complained about this, not without good reason. The big
men in the side—more than half the team—found being
hemmed in for long trips in constricting coach seats downright
uncomfortable. You can never do much reading in a coach,
unless you want to invite a headache. They couldn't play cards,
except rarely when they had a coach equipped with some tables.
They couldn't move around, as in a train, stretch their legs, go
to the buffet for a drink, meet people other than their team-
mates. This latter complaint was probably the worst aspect.
The coach travel made them introspective and this was
particularly bad after such things as losing a match and Murdoch being sent home. We don't need a psychiatrist to tell us
that the worst thing to do after a setback is to stew in your own
juice rather than get out and about with diversions to get
things off your mind.

Why was so much coach travel inflicted on them? It certainly
was not the fault of the agency in charge of travel arrangements.
In some cases the coach decision was forced on them through
the scrapping of many rail routes by Lord Beeching just after
the 1967 All Blacks' visit. In the Scottish Borders, for instance,
local trains do not exist any more. You travel by road or you
don't travel. But in the majority of cases the coach decision was
made by the New Zealand Rugby Council. In planning the
tour the travel agents presented them with alternatives by train
or coach (and sometimes plane) for the team's moves and it was
they who plumped for coach travel. In this they did the team a
disservice. They perhaps weren't to know that British Rail is
now much improved in some respects, that their Inter-City
services are a very agreeable, fast way to travel. In future tours
it is to be hoped for the players' sake that coach journeys are
kept down to a minimum.

With regard to 'indiscipline' . . . I travelled with the 1969
Springboks in the course of doing a book on their 'demo' tour
and it must be said that under extreme provocation they

showed highly commendable discipline and restraint. I doubt
very much whether these All Blacks would have been capable
of getting through a tour such as that without something
happening even more serious than the Murdoch affair.

Assistant Manager/Coach Duff being concerned mainly with
the training and playing activities of the side, the exercise of
discipline was chiefly in the charge of the other three members
of the management team—Manager Todd, captain Kirkpatrick and vice-captain Sid Going. They had their hands full,
as exemplified by Todd's Murdoch problems dealt with in the
next chapter.

Kirkpatrick's behaviour on and off the field was impeccable,
a model for the rest of the team. He was seen to indulge in only
one bit of retaliation, in one of the French matches at the close
of a frustrating tour, and who could blame him, when he was
being yanked out of a ruck in the grip of a vicious headlock?
His all round demeanour was in such contrast to those of the
team who did not appear to want to follow his example, as with
such incidents as Andy Haden coming off the pitch after the
North West Counties match and saying to the New Zealand
pressmen, 'What did you think of my king hit?', exulting over a
punch he had thrown.

Kirkpatrick the player lived right up to his reputation, an
automatic choice for any World XV as a loose forward. But not
as captain. I'm sure he would not want the job. It put years on
him, this tour. He might have had more help, in the sphere of
discipline, from his vice-captain.

There was question of the impact of Sid Going on the tour. It
was only a pity that it was not all on the credit side.

As a player Cliff Morgan called him 'half the All Black team'.
Each time he took the field he was undoubtedly determined to
imprint his name on the match. He could never have been
accused of being just a feeder of the backs. It was Pat Dwyer,
president of the New Zealand Rugby Union who put it in a nutshell to Terry McLean: 'I suppose we have to accept that Sid is
one of our greatest players and one of our poorer scrum-halves.'
To which McLean added the comment: 'He is a stunning
scrum-half—one of the very greatest. But if only he could pass!'

Going, for his part, said in an interview for *L'Equipe*: 'I have never neglected the importance of the pass. I have worked very hard in that sector. But to win a match, it is necessary that the forwards dominate. Therefore it is necessary for me to play to them.' Said Victor Boffelli, in a delightfully French remark: 'The All Black forwards never hide their admiration for Going. To them he is their Patron Saint.'

But, as can so often be the drawback of those who would impose their personality on a match, when Going was in top gear he was a match-winner but when he wasn't his solo breaks that didn't work, his kicks over his forwards' heads that weren't well placed made for much of the scrappy, untidy rugby that was to be seen too often from this side. Worse than that, being a focal point, much in the fray by his own choosing, his behaviour on the field was not, like Kirkpatrick's, beyond reproach.

Of the numerous Going incidents by far the most unsavoury was the flagrant punching in the East Glamorgan match which sent Gareth Evans to hospital for a two-hour operation on facial injuries. Off the field Going caused trouble within his own team as well as with those encountered outside—'a problem of the tour', as Terry McLean termed him. When the team was assembled in All Black off-the-field gear for the photography for their Christmas card, Going insisted on wearing a large Basque beret, something which has never featured in All Black uniforms, not in living memory at any rate. Self-conscious about balding, this was one of his pieces of cover-up headgear, like the Mafia-type black hat he had worn on arrival in Britain. No amount of persuasion would make him discard the beret for the team photo and the picture could not be used as intended. He was taciturn, uncommunicative, to the point of surliness. A Maori official at New Zealand House approached him at a social function, feeling they would strike a common chord since there aren't that many Maoris in England, but all he got from Going was a grunt. 'When I went up to him a second time at another party,' the official said, 'I only got another grunt, so I gave up.' When Going was captain in Kirkpatrick's absence against Cambridge University their captain, John Howard, felt hurt at receiving the same sort of grunt treatment from him before and after the match, to the university man hardly the off-the-field spirit of captains of opposing teams in rugby.

Going was accused of using a stronger version of 'Buzz off!' to photographers, autograph hunters and others who came to him unsolicited. Todd told the Press on his behalf that he was unhappy about this accusation, since he was a Mormon and Mormons never swear. That's true, of course. No Mormon ever uses profanity, just as no Catholic has ever been known to use a contraceptive.

It would be unfair to stand in judgment on Going for being taciturn and anti-social. It could be said that that is how he is by nature and that if he wanted to be that way on tour, it was no concern of anybody else. But unfortunately it was. He was vice-captain. Is it surprising, then, that young newcomers to touring in the party said to themselves, 'If the vice-captain acts like that, why shouldn't we?' Except that for them 'buzz off' was a bit mild.

In the latter stages of the tour the belated reinstating of the haka was not the only attempt made to make amends for the bad impression created with the British public. In other ways they strived, as a New Zealand paper put it, 'to set themselves on a higher road than they had previously managed to travel.' Sadly, however, the first impression is the one they will doubtless be labelled with when people here discuss them in the future. Especially as the Murdoch affair will always be there to trigger off reminiscences about the visit of the Seventh All Blacks.

LIFE BEGINS AT 40

Whatever was said about this debatable side, they at least established one record. When they beat Neath-Aberavon 43–3 they became the only touring side from overseas ever to pile up 40 points against a Welsh team—something such great tourists as the 1951 Springboks and Whineray's All Blacks never managed.

The closest any of their predecessors had ever come had been the 1924 All Blacks' 39–3 win over Swansea. And it was even closer to the magic 40-mark than the score indicates. They were cheated of their 40 by a technicality. As older rugby fans will remember, in those days a team-mate had to place the ball for you when you took a conversion, the instant the ball touched the ground being the moment at which the team waiting on the goal line could charge. When Mark Nicholls undertook the conversion of the All Blacks final try in front of the posts he thoughtlessly put the ball on the ground before digging his hole. Swansea regarded this as 'grounding the ball' and charged. The referee upheld them and Nicholls, surrounded by Swansea players, never had the chance to make the conversion which would have brought the total to 41 points.

It could be argued that by current scoring values the 1924 All Blacks' 39–3 against Swansea would have been 47–3, since they had scored nine tries, four conversions and a dropped goal. But why be niggardly and deny these latest All Blacks this little record of theirs?

SPREADING THE MESSAGE

The Welsh rarely let pass a good opportunity for some bible-banging. The evangelists were out in force among the captive audience to be found as the rugby fans accumulated outside Cardiff Arms Park prior to the Wales match with the All Blacks. One of the gentlemen drumming up trade for the Church had a placard on his back that proclaimed JESUS SAVES and he seemed quite unaware that someone had scrawled underneath 'He couldn't on my pay'.

PERSEVERANCE

Overheard at a rugby function during the course of the tour:
'He's written quite a few rugby books, hasn't he?'
'A lot.'
'Is he a good writer?'
'I don't know about him being a good writer but I do know that to get through one of his books you have to be a good reader.'

3

The Murdoch Affair

AT the outset of a tour, when you're writing a book on it, you take the earliest opportunity to familiarise yourself with each of the players. In the course of this procedure I approached Keith Murdoch.

'My name is Wallace Reyburn,' I said. 'I'm doing a book on the tour.'

'F—— off.'

One thing could be said for this exchange. At least we knew where we stood. From then on we were in amicable agreement. He went his way and I went mine.

I had emerged unscathed from that encounter with Murdoch, but others were less fortunate.

Ralph Sallon, longtime cartoonist for the *Daily Mirror*, had been commissioned to do caricatures of the players for a booklet on the tour being compiled by Terry Godwin. At a bar in the team's London hotel, the Britannia, he went around among them with his sketchpad. None raised any objection to posing for him until he came to Murdoch.

'If you try to do a f——ing drawing of me,' he said to Sallon, 'I'll f——ing well break your f——ing hand.'

He then set about putting his words into action. He seized Sallon's hand holding his pencil, clenched the fingers and pencil as in a vice and started bending the hand back. Acutely painful, permanent injury was only avoided by team-mates pulling Murdoch away. It was, characteristic of Murdoch, a quite unprovoked attack since Sallon could hardly have been accused of throwing his weight about. A little man, he is 73 years of age. Then, another characteristic of Murdoch to be observed during the Angel Hotel incident, he became obsessed with the cause of his annoyance and pursued Sallon all around the bar, until at length his friends in the team managed to pursuade him to call a halt.

Late one evening at the large, palatial Hydro Hotel, where the team were staying in Peebles, Murdoch went to the reception desk and said he would like his key.

'What name?' asked the man on duty.

'Whiting.'

'Which Whiting, sir?'

Murdoch was flummoxed.

What had happened was that he had heard someone say that Whiting was entertaining a girl in his room. It struck Murdoch that it would be great fun to burst in on them. (A favourite Murdoch lark; at another hotel he had tried to get hold of a pass key so that he could do it on a large scale.) But he had omitted to find out which Whiting it was, since there were two, Graham and Peter. So—when asked which Whiting, he was floored.

Also at the desk at the time to get his key was Norman Harris, a rugby writer for the *Sunday Times*. Not knowing anything of what had gone before and innocently seeking to clarify things for the clerk, Harris said 'This is Keith Murdoch.'

At which Murdoch turned on him, grasped him by the hair and threw him on the floor.

'You'd better f——ing watch out!' he shouted.

Murdoch did not know who Harris was and there could have been interesting repercussions had he instead been a Scottish laird or other similar guest of the type who use this first class hotel.

But Murdoch showed no fear or favour in his outbursts. At a social function for the All Blacks, Murdoch went after Sir William Ramsey, past president of the Rugby Football Union knighted for his services to the game. The air was blue with Murdoch's invective. Afterwards Sir William said that he had found Murdoch's vocabulary very limited and that he had told him he could beat him at swearing.

Murdoch cut a wide swath in his progress with the team through Britain and Northern Ireland. Passers-by outside the Dragon Hotel in Swansea were pelted with 'water bombs' (plastic bags filled with water) from a hotel window. More

messy was the experience of a young lady at a dance at the
Queen's Hotel in sedate Cheltenham who went out for some
fresh air at 1.30 a.m. and got doused with beer from a window
above. Doors off their hinges and other displays of strength
were commonplace at hotels at which the team stayed. At
Dunadry Inn outside Belfast detectives on special duty against
possible Irish troubles had their own sort of trouble with
Murdoch when they had to rush to his room to investigate a
chair which had gone smashing through the window.

All of which culminated in the affair at the Angel Hotel in
Cardiff, the outcome of which was the sending home of the 29-
year-old Murdoch, 17-stoner, man of many jobs—farm
worker, lorry driver, bar bouncer—the first All Black tourist
ever to have meted out to him that ultimate discipline.

The well-appointed Angel Hotel must be regarded as the best
in Cardiff, since the All Blacks on tour only stay at the best.
After the Wales match the Welsh Rugby Union always tender
an excellent dinner to the teams there and this is held in the
large balconied banqueting hall, approached from the lobby
through a long room with a bar occupying most of the length of
one side. After the dinner proper, friends, wives and girl
friends of the team members are allowed in to fill out the
evening drinking and chatting at the tables by the bar. As well
as the entrance from the lobby there is another directly from
the street and there are guards at these two entrances to keep
out would-be gate crashers of this highlight of the rugby
season. On the night of the dinner for these All Blacks there
were in all six guards at the hotel who had been supplied by
Qwent Security Services, a private firm with headquarters at
Newport.

At 12.30 Murdoch set the wheels in motion when he poured a
glass of beer over the head of a waiter. Apart from anything else,
this was an unwise thing to do since the bar was now shut and he
couldn't replace his drink. A waiter bearing a tray crammed
with empty glasses told him as much. He brought his elbow up
under the tray and sent the glasses flying. Security guards who
came to the spot were not only concerned about the disturb-
ance, they were worried about the danger of women in evening
shoes being cut by all the broken glass sprayed about.

Murdoch, with that characteristic of being obsessed with anyone who incurs his displeasure, chased the waiter into the kitchens. Security Officer Peter Grant and another guard followed. Team-mates of Murdoch joined the melee that developed, trying to restrain him. The waiter was hustled from the kitchens and sent upstairs to his room for safety. The banqueting manager was called. Team manager Ernie Todd was summoned. Todd said to Murdoch: 'We've had enough trouble from you already. If you don't behave yourself you'll be sent home.' The two guards took the gesture Murdoch made towards his manager as an attempt to hit him and they moved in. Four men in all were occupied in trying to subdue Murdoch, two from behind and the two guards in front trying to pin down the massive flailing arms of Murdoch. 'It was like trying to control two whirling telegraph poles,' they said afterwards.

Before things quietened down five security officers and other All Blacks were in the kitchens. At length Murdoch's colleagues said that they could handle him and the guards withdrew.

Peter Grant, himself not a small man at 17 stone and 6 ft 4 in, described what happened next: 'As we were coming out of the kitchen Murdoch shouted at me, "You IRA bastard!" I'm not even an Irishman. I come from Nuneaton. Then I was out near the bar talking to one of the other players. I thought Murdoch had gone by then. But all of a sudden—clock! He struck me from behind a pillar with a right-hander that gave me a left-eye shiner. I'm reasonably big but this bloke Murdoch had hands like shovels and his arms and wrists make mine look like matchsticks. It was a blow that might have killed a smaller man. I was dazed but ready to have a go at him. Fortunately other security men held me back. They probably thought all hell would break loose if they let me go.'

Already enough hell had broken loose for the police to be called and they asked Grant whether he wanted to lay any charges. 'Yes!' said Grant, not unnaturally in a worked-up state. But when the scene moved to the local police station he had subsided and was in the mood to take a more charitable view of the matter. He told the police he would not proceed against Murdoch.

However, Murdoch's activity did not end there. He was to be

observed at 4 o'clock in the morning in the corridors of the hotel with a handkerchief as an improvised bandage over a bloodied fist. Four doors could be seen to have sustained damage. He was locked, alone, in the room of captain Ian Kirkpatrick. Afterwards the room could not be occupied again until the numerous breakages were repaired or replaced.

Team manager Ernie Todd was busily engaged that Sunday with telephone calls and personal conferences with representatives of, among others, the hotel management, the security firm, the Welsh Rugby Union, the Press and—most importantly—the body to which he was directly responsible, the New Zealand Rugby Council, and the hosts of his team in Britain, the Tours Committee of the Four Home Rugby Unions.

He made a statement to the effect that Murdoch was being disciplined, but would not say precisely what form the discipline would take. It seemed logical that, as happened when Colin Meads of the 1967 All Blacks was sent off against Scotland and he was suspended for two matches, something similar would be meted out to Murdoch. But it seemed that that was not going to be the case. Murdoch's name was announced among those to play West Midlands at Moseley on the following Wednesday. As far as Todd would go was to say that he had given Murdoch 'a bloody good talking to'.

And on that note the affair appeared to have been closed when the All Blacks were established on that Sunday in their new hotel, the Strathallan in Birmingham.

But on Monday morning things happened fast. At 10 a.m. the whole team assembled in their coach outside the hotel to go for training. As they were about to pull off, however, a bellboy ran from the hotel to tell Murdoch that Todd wanted to see him. The team waited and shortly Murdoch emerged again. He got his gear from the coach and with a wave of his hand to the other players said 'Hooray, boys' and started back towards the hotel. (For the sake of those unfamiliar with New Zealand slang, 'hooray' for some reason means 'goodbye'.)

Later Todd was to say that captain Kirkpatrick and vice-captain Sid Going, as co-members with himself and coach Bob Duff of the management four, were kept fully informed at every step of the way as to what was happening. But this did not seem to tally with the fact that Kirkpatrick now got out of the coach and chased after Murdoch. He questioned him and then shook him by the hand before watching him go into the hotel.

The news was now out. Murdoch had been sent home. For the players training became secondary and they piled out of the coach. In the hotel lobby they learned that Murdoch had been given three-quarters of an hour to get his things together, turn in his All Black insignia and then, escorted by Stanley Couchman, Rugby Football Union liaison officer with the team, take train to London and thence to Heathrow airport to be put on a plane New Zealand bound. This shattering news clearly affected his team-mates. Haden burst into tears. They all wanted to go up to Murdoch's seventh-floor room, shared by Lin Colling, to bid him farewell. So many crowded into the lift that it got stuck.

When Murdoch came down, dressed in open-neck shirt, All Black issue grey trousers and now anonymous black blazer, and was being taken out through the lobby one of the New Zealand photographers shot a picture. Murdoch, in the style of someone being ushered from court, put up a hand to cover his face. 'I'd rather you didn't print that photo,' Todd said to the photographer.

In the fourth-floor team room Todd gave a Press conference, at which there were nine British and New Zealand correspondents. He said that the decision, for the good of Murdoch and for the good of the team as a whole, was his alone.

'Keith was magnificent,' he said. 'He took it on the chin. He did not say one word of reproach. He was dedicated to our team cause. He would have given anything—he gave everything—to help us. When you have dedicated men like that, you have the real core of rugby men.'

One felt that in the field of oddly worded official statements this would take its place as a collector's item. Was Murdoch in a position to reproach *anybody?* Any young player aspiring to be a dedicated team man would hardly be advised to take Murdoch's behaviour at the Angel Hotel as a model.

On arrival at London's Euston station Murdoch was whisked acrosstown to the offices of T. H. Hamer (Passenger Agents) Ltd, the firm in charge of travel arrangements for this tour, as on many previous tours. They are, appropriately enough, at 7 Haymarket, right opposite New Zealand House. Murdoch was kept hidden there for two hours, with a hired Rolls-Royce on hand to take him to the airport.

To while away the time waiting the chauffeur brought an *Evening Standard*. Across the front page was a banner headline, 'WILD MAN' SENT HOME, a large picture of Murdoch and a story by Barry Newcombe occupying most of the front page's reading matter. When Murdoch was brought out to the car the chauffeur showed him the *Standard* and he grunted his acknowledgement of being the man who had made rugby for the first time ever the front page lead in a major British newspaper.

At Heathrow, Murdoch's luggage for flight QF744 was put through by proxy and although those who got him to his plane did a wonderful job of what they termed 'helping Murdoch escape public embarrassment', the British Airports Authority took a different view of such VIP treatment. They felt called upon to institute an inquiry into how Murdoch was smuggled out, who gave permission for him to be spirited through the inwards hall instead of the departure hall and straight to the waiting Qantas jumbo jet ahead of the 300 other passengers.

There was naturally tremendous interest in New Zealand in the return of Murdoch but he frustrated the reception committee of rugby officials and newsmen by jumping the plane at Darwin. Unheard from for two months, he at length cabled his mother in Dunedin to the effect that he was staying on in Australia's Northern Territory. Ernie Todd's handling of the whole affair could hardly be termed incisive. Many wondered why Murdoch on the day after the incident was apparently pardoned (since he was chosen for the next match) and then next day abruptly banished from the touring party. Asked for an explanation of this sudden switch-around, Todd said: 'I had to check two points and then I was forced to reconsider.' He doubtless meant it figuratively, but there was reason to believe that 'forced to reconsider' could be taken literally.

Forced by whom?

The Angel Hotel management (Tom Carroll, manager, and Ian Norton, assistant manager) bore no grudge. They went on record as saying that these were the occupational hazards when rugby teams visited them; what had happened was no worse than their experience with local teams; it had been blown up out of all proportion because it was the All Blacks. And the hotel's forgive-and-forget attitude was borne out by their welcoming the team for two further stays later in the tour.

The Gwent Security Services? Like the hotel, they brought no pressure to bear. Jack Powell, head of the firm, told me that a rumour which circulated was quite unfounded. The theory was that Security Officer Peter Grant was going to go ahead with his initial intention of charging Murdoch with assault. To have a member of the touring side involved in court proceedings would have been of untold embarrassment to the rugby authorities here and in New Zealand, so (the rumour had it) a deal had been made whereby Grant would drop the charges if Murdoch was sent home. 'There was absolutely no truth in that,' said Powell.

From only two sources could pressure have come that would have forced Todd to change from apparent leniency to a show of firmness. There seems little doubt that his bosses, the New Zealand Rugby Council, and his hosts, the Tours Committee of the Four Home Unions, felt that 'a bloody good talking to' hardly fitted the seriousness of the offence.

At the end of the tour when Todd himself was leaving for home he said in an interview with Terry O'Connor of the *Daily Mail*: 'I would like to say now that it was always my intention to send Murdoch home following the Cardiff punch-up, but told a white lie to give me time to complete travel arrangements.'

This may have been accepted by the general reader, but not by anyone who took the trouble to check with Qantas Airways as to how difficult it had been to get air passage to New Zealand at that time. A spokesman for the airline told me: 'Not only was there plenty of space available on flight QF744, the one Murdoch took on the Monday. We could easily have accepted him as a passenger on flight QF742 on the Sunday evening. It went out with 11 empty seats.'

Murdoch's team-mates had been cast into depression by his abrupt removal. Their low morale contributed to their inability to ward off defeat on their next match. With anybody who would listen they went to Murdoch's defence. They pointed out that nobody, not even Murdoch, liked being referred to as 'a bloody animal', a comment which had been heard to come from the direction of the security officers at the Angel Hotel. They claimed that it takes two to make a fight, that Peter Grant had been aggressive. Jack Powell's comment on this assertion was: 'Peter does have a formidable presence. It instils in the average person a feeling of "I don't think I'll chance it".' One might agree with the view that it takes two to make a fight when two 17-stone fit men both trained to use their size and weight (the one as a prop forward and the other as a security officer) come face to face.

New Zealand correspondents with the team were quick to send stories home listing what they claimed were examples of aggressiveness by security officers at the hotel. In support of the contention that Grant had had much to do with the contretemps developing into a blood-letting punch-up, the pro-All Black faction stated shortly after the affair that Grant was no longer in the employ of Gwent Security. This was quite untrue. Powell could assure anybody who asked that Grant was still a valued employee of the firm.

But whether or not personal animosity had developed between the two men was not the main issue. Even Murdoch's most ardent supporters could have no defence for things he did before and after that confrontation.

Todd's high praise for Murdoch after his banishment—'he was magnificent . . . he took it like the wonderful man he is'— came under the heading of being charitable, not hitting him when he was down. But the crux of the whole thing was that Murdoch should have been hit when he was up, i.e. he should have been passed over in the selection of the team to come to Britain. It was all very well for a selector to say: 'We need a bit of knuckle to sort things out in the front row.' In the cliche phrase, members of a touring team are ambassadors for their country.

There have always been rough diamonds in any All Black touring side. Did not one member of the 1924 tourists drop his false teeth in his soup while in conversation with the Princess Royal at a dinner? The art of All Black team selection lies in eliminating from consideration anyone liable to step over the narrow dividing line between being awarded the CSE while on overseas duty (Constant Source of Embarrassment) and being stupid enough to punch people—off the field.

The selectors knew that Murdoch had been involved in brawls when with the 1970 All Blacks in South Africa. They must shoulder the blame for not having the wisdom to decide that his value as a player was far outweighed by the certainty that in Britain he would again be the focal point of trouble when relaxing from his activities on the field.

MURDOCH THE GARDENER

Before things went sour there were Murdoch jokes. (There's one hidden among the statistics, which went to press before the rest of this book.) A Murdoch joke I liked concerned someone telling a friend what a strong man he was. 'I went past Murdoch's house the other day and saw him clipping his hedge.' 'Who doesn't clip his hedge?' said his friend. To which the reply was: 'With a power mower?'

POETIC LICENCE

Harsh comment about the performance of John Davies, fullback for Cardiff against the All Blacks:
'They call him the Ancient Mariner.'
'Why?'
'He stoppeth one of three.'

THE TARNISHED MEDAL

For many years now the Welsh have been wearing like a medal the fact that Wales have beaten the All Blacks three times. But that medal has become more than a little tarnished now, in view of their defeat by these Seventh All Blacks. It means that they have lost their last five games against New Zealand on the trot. Their moments of glory against the New Zealanders were away back in 1905, 1935 and 1953.

Llanelli having beaten the All Blacks, we now have the situation whereby Welsh clubs over the years have a better record against them than their national side—four victories (by Llanelli, Swansea, Cardiff and Newport).

And an interesting fact emerges if we look at the record of the four home countries against those two giants from down south— the All Blacks and the Springboks. Wales never having beaten the Springboks (the only major rugby country never to have pulled it off), her record against these two great rivals is now no better than that of England and Scotland. In fact all three countries have had precisely the same measure of success:

	Wins v NZ	Wins v SA	Draws v NZ	Draws v SA	Totals
Wales	3	–	–	1	3 wins, 1 draw
England	1	2	–	1	–ditto–
Scotland	–	3	1	–	–ditto–

(Ireland have had a win and a draw against South Africa, a draw against New Zealand.)

GUINNESS CHANGES THE RECORDS

Best-seller among the books the tourists bought while they were over here was the *Guinness Book of Records*. They were a little bewildered, though, when they looked up RUGBY and saw that South Africa's famous win over Scotland in 1952 was by a margin of 53–0 and not 44–0 as is generally accepted, that New Zealand's trouncing of Northern NSW in 1962 was 125–0, not 102–0 as we all thought, plus numerous other radical differences from what all the rugby books say. It looked like blatant errors . . . until they noticed a little note in italics, to the effect that 'all point scores have been compiled according to current values.'

When you think about it, this is such a stupid thing to do that I could not help but phone Ross McWhirter, boss with brother Norris of the *Guinness* book, and ask him what on earth had possessed them to make such a boo-boo. At least I tried to phone Ross McWhirter. It was at the time of his successful seeking of an injunction momentarily banning the TV film about Andy Warhol and he was receiving so many abusive phone calls that the Post Office had stepped in to make his number unobtainable. So I phoned brother Norris.

Although they hadn't been directly responsible for those changes, it hadn't dawned on him how assinine it had been to let the scores be tampered with. You see, if you start changing past scores to bring them in line with current values, you're going to change the *results* of a lot of matches. To give just one of hundreds of examples. . . . That memorable 3–3 draw between England and Scotland in 1965 when Scotland, leading by a dropped goal, saw England pull level in the dying minutes through Andy Hancock's sensational try. If, as *Guinness* have it, the Springboks scored 53 and not 44 against Scotland in 1962, then England didn't just draw against them in 1965—they beat them 4–3.

Norris McWhirter assured me all would be back to normal in their next edition.

4

Some Assessments

Trevor Morris. His was the saddest story of the tour. A youngster of what Alex Vesey described as 'towering ability', he had played a great game in a Trial as far back as 1964. But the selectors never seemed to get around to following this through and developing him in big-time rugby. It didn't help that he wasn't playing regularly in one of the shop-window locales such as Auckland, say, or Christchurch. How can you catch anybody's eye in Motueka? Also the full-back slot for New Zealand when Morris was in his early twenties was in the capable hands of Don Clarke, then Williment and McCormick. But then, in his late twenties, he was the surprise selection for the All Blacks' internal tour at the start of the New Zealand 1972 season. He confounded his critics. He did so well he was automatic choice as full-back in all three Tests against the visiting Wallabies. And thence straight into the All Blacks for this tour, as undoubtedly No. 1 New Zealand full-back.

Great feeling to be recognised at last, and packing his bags to come over here he could be excused for dreaming of moments of glory on the rugby pitches of Britain and France, to wind up (wonderful thought) taking his place among the greats who had come before . . . Billy Wallace, George Nepia, Bob Scott, Don Clarke. . . .

He had the equipment to do it. A wonderful touch-finder with either foot, big incisive punts. A very sound tackler. An acknowledged exponent of the long drop-kick. An 'attacking full-back', effective at joining in with the other backs. Place-kicking ability that had brought him 75 points on the short internal tour. And to cap it all, the touch of class in the way he went about his business.

So all was set for a great tour.

But in one of the warm-up games in North America on the way over he sustained a leg injury. Not too serious, it was announced on the team's arrival in Britain . . . Karam would fill in for him in the opening match. But the injury lingered on. It was not until the eighth match that he made his British debut. The confidence wasn't there. It didn't look as though he'd be ready in time to take over his rightful place in the first Test, against Wales. And what happened in *that* game? Karam was the match-winner. And the better Karam got the worse Morris seemed to fare. His place-kicking became the subject of crowd ridicule. Like a Test cricketer trying for that big innings to reinstate himself, like Tony Jacklin trying to get his putting right and back into the big money, Morris fought to restore his self-assurance. But gradually he was running out of matches to do it in, with Karam even more firmly establishing himself as New Zealand's new No. 1 full-back.

Sadly the time came when Morris had to be written off as one of the failures of the tour. In the eighth of his meagre number of appearances he *did* kick the penalty which saved the All Blacks against Munster. But what a small crumb of solace that is to look back on when at the outset you had every right to hope that by tour's end you'd be numbered among the great full-backs that New Zealand has sent to Europe.

Joe Karam. In the course of his first outing as a full All Black, against British Columbia at Vancouver, a ball landed in front of Karam and bounced into his hands. 'Mark!' he exclaimed, surprisingly. 'Ye Gods,' his team-mates said to themselves, 'what sort of a no-hoper have we got here? But it doesn't matter. We've got Morris. We'll be able to hide this Karam in the lesser mid-week matches.'

It was very much on this basis of 'Why was he ever picked?' that the 20-year-old of Lebanese extraction started the tour proper. And it was by dint of his conscientious application and his determination to do well that in the eyes of the British crowds he matured with every match from 'This boy's not bad' to 'My God, he's good!'

Not spectacular—none of the flair of Bob Scott or the awesome presence of Don Clarke—his success could be summed up in one word—reliability. Rarely did one see him make a mistake in handling, tackling or touch-finding. His place-kicking was so sound that he reached his century in his 14th match—it took Clarke 16 outings to get his 'ton' when he was over here and Scott (19 matches in 1953-4) never did make it!

A classic straight-on kicker—so much more pleasing to watch than the dicey round-the-corner merchants—he was said to be a protege of Clarke. In actual fact he met him but once, when he was 14-years-old and attended a Rothman's coaching session at which the Master was giving tips to young-sters. 'He told me two things,' Karam says. 'Keep your head down and follow through. And I have those imprinted on my mind whenever I go up to kick.'

Normally on the morning of a match the selected XV doesn't train, only the 'dirt-trackers' (those of the touring party not chosen). But typical of Karam's dedication was that he would be out there with them before each match with a batch of balls, banging away at the goal posts for more than an hour.

Highwater mark of his kicking performances was the Wales Test, in which he played Penalty Ping-pong with Phil Bennett and beat him 5 to 4. A coach might say that those 15 points, Karam's highest match total on the tour, just go to show the value to a place-kicker of a pre-match warm-up . . . except that on this particular occasion he went on to the field cold, the All Blacks having arrived in Cardiff too late for him to have his usual morning session.

Likeable, self-effacing. One feels he'll stay the same when he gets back home and the adulation of this new All Black hero gets under way. After all, he has earned it. He scored in every match in which he played and his total of 138 points for the tour was higher than the great Don Clarke's 136 in 1963-4. In fact Karam scored more individual points than any other All Black tourist in Europe since Billy Wallace's record 214 for the First All Blacks away back in 1905!

Bryan Williams. This was the known crowd-pleaser of the side, the exciting personality everyone was looking forward to seeing in action again. When he came to England in 1971 as a guest for the centenary matches his reputation had preceded him. 'Best winger in the world,' said the South Africans after his tour there with the 1970 All Blacks. 'A genius—and I use the

THE 1972-73 ALL BLACKS IN THE BRITISH ISLES AND FRANCE

Back Row (*left to right*): R. E. Burgess, B. G. Williams, R. W. Norton, B. J. Robertson, K. K. Lambert, I. N. Stevens; **Third Row**: R. M. Parkinson, J. D. Matheson, K. W. Stewart, R. A. Urlich, A. J. Wyllie, M. Sayers, K. Murdoch; **Second Row**: A. I. Scown, I. M. Eliason, H. H. Macdonald, A. M. Haden, P. J. Whiting, A. R. Sutherland, G. J. Whiting, B. Holmes; **Front Row**: E. L. Todd (manager), T. J. Morris, S. M. Going (vice-capt.), I. A. Kirkpatrick (capt.), G. R. Skudder, I. A. Hurst, R. H. Duff (assistant manager); **In Front**: G. L. Colling, G. B. Batty, D. A. Hales, J. F. Karam.

GRANT BATTY: STAR OF THE TOUR

'Dynamite' Batty, as the French called the All Black winger, started the tour as an unknown and wound up the team's greatest crowd pleaser. Devastating runner, ramrod tackler, he scored 19 tries. (*Above*) He is on his way in typical style to one of his four against Cambridge. (*Below*) Although the camera distorts, Batty really was tiny at 5 ft 5½ ins compared to Western Counties lock Watt (No. 4) as he is seen here brilliantly wrong-footing the Counties' backs.

JOE KARAM: SURPRISE SUCCESS

It was purely by chance that the inexperienced Karam got a lot of early games through injury to first-string full-back Morris. The ever reliable Mini-Gibraltar Karam matured with every match, made himself New Zealand's undoubted No. 1 full-back. His 138 points was the highest individual total for an All Black in Europe since Billy Wallace of the 1905 side. (*Above*) He is seen recording the tour's most unusual score – the 'hood-wink try', when he dashed for the line against London Counties instead of taking the expected shot at goal.

word with full responsibility,' wrote Terry McLean. And
Williams fully lived up to this high praise when he showed his
paces with the RFU President's Overseas XV at Twickenham
and elsewhere in '71.

When the All Blacks arrived for this tour the only worry about
him was—would the New Zealanders get the ball out to him
enough to make the most of his speed and brilliant side-
stepping ability? In the opening match against Western
Counties they served notice that they fully intended to. He
scored three tries, made two others and just missed scoring his
fourth. What a feast we were in for from this marvellous
runner with the ball!

But then things went flat. Williams straightway went into
such an arid patch that when the halfway mark of the tour had
been reached he had managed to add merely one more try to
his burst of scoring in that first match. And as the rest of the
tour unfolded, tries didn't seem to come any more easily for him.

He most certainly wasn't a failure on this tour. Not for one
moment would one say that he played badly. But the unhappy
thing for him was that constantly he was being outshone by a
young newcomer over on the other wing. . . .

Grant Batty. They called him a terrier, a fizzing firecracker, the human catapult, the mini-dynamo, the pocket
battleship. The rugby writers vied with each other in trying to
put in a nutshell the exhilarating presence of this little winger
who enlivened every game he played in. Unknown at the start
of the tour, he built his reputation so fast that in no time each
crowd was just waiting for the ball to come his way. Invariably
it didn't take long, because the most apt term to apply to Batty
was 'competitive'. He always wanted to be in there where the
action was, whether on attack or defence, as against the more
conventional Williams, who usually played the traditional
winger's role of waiting for the ball to reach him. Batty made so
many of his chances. And this had much to do with the fact that
when he scored his 14th try, against East Midlands, and one
looked up the Williams tries one saw that it was precisely half
that tally in the same number of appearances. And sad to say
the Williams' total was to stay at seven for the whole tour,
while Batty's jumped to 19.

Batty's speed, with what were inevitably called 'his egg-beater legs', was such that one felt that more than once a referee ruled him offside when following up a kick on the basis that no one could possibly have got there in such short order.

At 5 ft 5½ ins, Batty is the most diminutive three-quarter ever to have represented New Zealand and as much of a joy to watch as his electrifying runs was his tackling, a sphere in which, at a mere 11 st, he was giving away as much as 5 st to forwards like Delme Thomas and even to three-quarters such as England's Warfield conceding 3 st. But he brought them down, always bigger men than he, because his was the copybook rugby tackle, in which 'the shoulder goes into the thigh and the encircling arms strangle the legs above the knee'. And if ever there was an object lesson that 'the victim is not dragged down —he is literally knocked over by the impact', Batty provided it. On numerous occasions there was spontaneous applause at the sight of a ball-carrier going flat out not merely being stopped in his tracks but being abruptly propelled several yards backwards by the force of the Batty impact.

When he himself headed for the line he had an almost fanatical determination not to be impeded. Which brings up a couple of his shortcomings, which must be mentioned before this sounds too much like a handout from the Batty Fan Club. On the field he was a petulant little chap. He might argue that this stemmed from jersey pulling and other obstruction used to try to curb him. But the fact remains that he was often inclined to turn nasty at close quarters. The key to this, I should think, is contained in the name of the Wellington club he plays for— Marists-St. Pat's. For what reason I do not know, there appears to be a link in New Zealand rugby between Catholic schools and clubs and dirty play. I remember in my youth encounters on the rugby field playing against Auckland's Sacred Heart and Marist Brothers. After such games one felt one's balls had been through the wringer.

The other Batty shortcoming was mucking around getting the ball thrown in to a line-out and it could be argued that he lost the game for the All Blacks against North West Counties by conceding a penalty for one such delayed throw-in.

But having mentioned those faults, let's return to Batty's

praise. Unquestionably the star of the tour, he is the best thing that has happened to New Zealand rugby for many a year.

George Skudder. A friendly, popular tourist, Skudder had leg trouble which delayed his debut in Britain and then the strapping he had to wear on the field did nothing to help his mobility. That's probably the kindest way of summing up his performance on tour. He showed the occasional flash of brilliance on attack but that could hardly compensate for his being a liability on defence and his general lack of class. He had had one Test when he came over. One would be hard put to visualise his ever having another.

Bruce Robertson. Although injury created an unfortunate gap in his early appearances, this 20-year-old eventually lived up to his mini-reputation in New Zealand before the tour. A big, strong runner in the centre, a superb solo try against Scotland was the highlight of his visit.

Ian Hurst, brought over as a second-string centre, was another of the 'surprise choices' which the selectors are forced to indulge in with such a dearth of good backs in New Zealand. Just 20 and a complete unknown before the tour, he did extremely well considering his lack of big-time experience. So much so that he was tried at second five-eighth alongside first-string centre Bruce Robertson and prospered, managing to oust **Mike Parkinson,** regular Test man in that position, for the last two Internationals.

I suppose Hurst could be regarded as one of the successes of the tour, to the extent that we'll probably hear more of him in the future.

Duncan Hales. For the Internal Tour by the All Blacks at the start of the 1972 season Hales was what they're fond of calling in New Zealand 'a surprise choice'—in other words, 'We've got Williams on one wing, who on earth can we stick on the other?' He did well enough in those domestic matches to be picked as Williams' co-wing in the three Tests against the Wallabies and it was expected that over here he would consolidate himself as regular N.Z. winger. He didn't. Grant Batty saw to that. But as luck would have it, as far as Hales was concerned, injuries to midfield backs meant that he got numerous games as a centre, six on the trot as a matter of fact, including a

Test (against Wales). But with Robertson and Hurst restored to health he took on the role of a midweek winger, to return to New Zealand as one of the forgettables, of which this team contained a high proportion.

Ian Stevens, Mark Sayers. . . . Having waxed enthusiastic at the beginning of this chapter about new boys Karam and Batty, it becomes increasingly difficult to go on down the line of this batch of youngsters New Zealand sent over as a back division and elevate them, by detailed comment, to men of stature. At the outset of the tour an English Rugby Union official said to me: 'Ask the Lions what they think of New Zealand backs, they think they're a joke.' That's a bit hard but, looking at it quite objectively, can one really speak in the same breath of the backs Britain sent to New Zealand in 1971 and these young visitors?

New Zealand backplay has certainly reached a sorry state when at this stage in the game's history there the best the selectors can do is choose a batch of kids like these and keep their fingers crossed that some of them come good. Karam did and Batty did. But viewing the general picture of the All Blacks' backplay on this tour who will deny that it was tentative, immature and lacking in authority? And now that the tour is over one must confess that these young hopefuls are about as interesting to read about, and write about, as the life story of the second guitarist in a newly formed pop group.

Bob Burgess. To keep his flowing locks under control Burgess played with a band on. Everyone was unhappy that he didn't more often play with abandon. When he did run with the ball it was sheer poetry. Not with a jink but a glide, he'd slice through the opposite side. Perhaps most memorable were his two almost identical tries against Neath/Aberavon. Each time his slinking run took him in a beautiful curve through the opposing line without anyone able to lay a hand on him. There were other tries and breaks he made which bore the same stamp of a fly-half of the highest standard.

But not often enough, as far as onlookers were concerned, did he give full rein to his exciting ability as a runner with the ball. It was not of his choosing that this was so. When paired with Going he had so often to stand by and watch him playing his

9-man rugby and then, when favoured with a pass from Going, he was forced to adhere to the much liked tactical policy of these All Blacks—the high punt. However, when in combination with Colling, not only did he get a friendly stream of good passes but also, released from the Little Man's influence, he could play with a sense of freedom. It speaks for itself that the big scores came when Burgess and Colling were together, that in the matches in which they were paired the New Zealand backs scored 27 tries, as against merely 11 when it was Burgess-Going.

Lin Colling's pass was one of the best things to watch on the tour. A scrum-half dedicated to setting his backs in motion, he had the long, accurate spin pass to give them the best possible type of getaway. A reflection of his friendliness with the backs was the fact that the three big scores of the tour (the 39 and the two 43s) were piled up when he was in action. However. . . .

The three provincial defeats, most there had ever been on an All Black tour of Britain, all came when he was scrum-half. Which prompts the interesting query: if he is to be given the credit for the open rugby that produced those big scores, should his style of play also be blamed for those three disasters? It's hard to say. Best thing to do would be to ask Ian Kirkpatrick. He was skipper on the field in all three of those matches.

Sid Going, Ian Kirkpatrick and **Keith Murdoch** we deal with more fully elsewhere.

Peter Whiting. After the Wales Test, Delme Thomas said: 'Peter Whiting is a superb line-out man.' After the Scotland Test, Peter Brown said: 'You can get nowhere until you neutralise him in the line-out.' After the first match in France at Tarbes the most capped (50) Frenchman, Benoit Dauga, said: 'I've recognised today the best lock in the world. He surpasses all others I've seen. Peter Whiting has no equal in the line-out.'

And who better to judge at first hand than they?

As exhilarating to watch as his line-out work was a ploy he and Karam practised and were eminently successful with at kick-offs and restarts from the centre spot. Going like a bomb, the 6 ft 6 in Whiting would leap up to Karam's lofted kick-off and high above the heads of the waiting opponents flick it cleanly back for All Black possession. Adapted from his basketball activities, this Whiting speciality was wonderful to watch but ironically it was something New Zealand supporters hoped he would have as few opportunities as possible to bring into play.

One of the outstanding successes of the tour.

Kent Lambert. When you're just turned 20 it's great to be picked for the Big One—a tour of Britain and France. But with experienced props like Murdoch, Matheson and Graham Whiting along on the tour you knew there was little chance of getting into the Test side. You were just the youngster with 'a promising future' whom the selectors hoped would profit by the experience and eventually be Test material.

But in only the second International, against Scotland, Lambert's 'promising future' came rushing to meet him. Matheson had to come off with the injury that finished his tour. Murdoch had already been sent home. What other prop was there available to trot out on to Murrayfield to join Graham Whiting?

It was one of those lucky breaks that come only now and then to a 'new boy'. For example, such good fortune didn't attend the other youngster among the forwards, 19-year-old **Ken Stewart.** The other loose forwards he'd come over with remained stubbornly free of major injury.

Much to Lambert's credit he made the most of his lucky break and kept his Test place despite the arrival of prop replacements.

Alex Wyllie. As far back as when the selected team for the tour was announced, the British Press went after 'bad boy Wyllie'. The happenings at the notorious Lions-Canterbury match were rehashed. There was 'surprise that the All Black selectors have chosen a man of such ill repute'.

But as the tour progressed this 27-year-old flanker didn't seem to be such a terrible person after all. On the field and off the 'bad boy' tag wasn't all that appropriate. He was a very good team man, a great old organiser, tickets and that sort of thing. And the three times he was called upon to be captain (against Edinburgh & Glasgow, Combined Services and

Munster), the Press found themselves calling up words of praise.

One wondered about Kirkpatrick returning home with his team that hadn't lived up to New Zealand's high standards. The knives would be out. Perhaps it wouldn't be long before we'd be seeing '(capt.)' after the name of the greatly matured Wyllie.

Alistair Scown. A volatile loose forward, one of the finds of the Test series against the 1972 Wallabies, Scown appropriately enough often had something between a scowl and a frown on his face, feeling hard done by at being passed over for major appearances on this tour. But with the heavier, more abrasive Kirkpatrick, Wyllie and **Alan Sutherland** playing in top form, where to fit him in?

Ian Eliason, Bevan Holmes, Andy Haden. Every tour, sad to say, has players such as these—the type of which at the beginning of the tour onlookers ask 'Who's he?' and they're still saying it by tour's end. Young lock Haden, however, looks less likely than the other two to take the quick road to rugby oblivion on returning home. He was often prominent in the loose and might well have become a Test man on this tour had it not been for the presence of the outstanding Peter Whiting and the less spectacular but hard-working **Hamish Macdonald.**

IN THE FOG

Who qualifies as the Wit of the Pressbox? My vote would go to Clem Thomas, of the *Observer*. I liked his story about Llanelli being hosts to the Barbarians and the local crowd being so disgusted with the poor rugby that they were turning on that day that there came a voice from the crowd: 'Go back to Barbaria!'

This may well have been derivitive but entirely on the spur of the moment was his comment during the All Blacks' match with East Glamorgan, played in a fog so dense that all one could see were wraith-like figures occasionally emerging from the gloom. Said Thomas: 'I'm going to need a ghost writer for this game.'

BRIEF INTERLUDE

The Permissive Society, about which we have heard so much, has penetrated to the rugby world. In the old days when a player's shorts came adrift and a new pair were brought on, a modesty screen was formed around him by his team-mates while he changed and the discarded pair were, by tradition, tossed out from the huddle ('Ha! Ha! Ha!' from the crowd). It's all different now.

When Sid Going ripped his in the London Counties match and a new pair were brought to him he changed right out there in the open. In front of the Royal Box. (Unoccupied at the time, praise be to heaven.)

For the record: he wears bright red jockey-shorts.

CONTRIBUTION

Acid remark about the All Blacks' 43-point slaughter of Neath-Aberavon: 'One thing that must be said for the Neath-Aberavon side. They did make their contribution to the match. They turned up.'

NOISES OFF

The rugby authorities were disturbed by the increasing tendency, when place-kickers of the visiting side were taking shots at goal, for certain elements at rugby grounds not to accord them the traditional silence but instead plague them with whistles and catcalls. Over the public address system at Cardiff Arms Park an official admonished them for such behaviour and asked them to desist. Laudatory, but inconsistent. Why did he not also admonish the section of Welsh crowds which gave the same sort of treatment to the playing of *God Save the Queen?*

What effect did it actually have on the place-kickers? Who better to say than Joe Karam, who on this tour had the best record of success with place kicks of any All Black since Billy

Wallace of the First All Blacks in 1905?

'I'd hear the noise when I was placing the ball but then when I was walking back and doing my run-up I was so busy concentrating that I became unaware of it and it had no affect on me at all.'

PART TWO

The Matches

In May and June of the New Zealand 1972 season there was an internal tour by an All Black side:

All Blacks beat	N.Z. Juniors	25– 9
	Marlborough	59–10
	Mid-Canterbury	52– 7
	Southland	30– 9
	Wanganui	39–21
	Counties	42– 8
	North Auckland	33–15
	Wairarapa-Bush	38– 0
	Manawatu	37– 9

Played 9, won 9. Points for: 355, against: 88.

In July and August, Australia toured New Zealand, three of their 13 matches being Tests:

August 19, 1972:   New Zealand beat Australia 29– 6
September 2, 1972: New Zealand beat Australia 30–17
September 12, 1972: New Zealand beat Australia 38– 3

On the way over to Europe the 1972–3 All Blacks played two matches in North America:

Brockton Oval, Vancouver, October 19, 1972: All Blacks beat British Columbia 31–7. Tries: Burgess (2), Kirkpatrick (2), Batty, Robertson. Penalty: Karam. Conversions: Karam (2).

Downing Stadium, New York, October 21, 1972: All Blacks beat New York All Stars 41–9. Tries: Sutherland (2), Batty (penalty try), Macdonald, Hurst, Wyllie, Going, Lambert. Penalty: Williams. Conversions: Williams, Morris, Going.

Western Counties

Kingsholm, Gloucester, Saturday, October 28, 1972
Attendance: 17,000

Teams and Scorers

All Blacks		Western Counties		
Karam	4C P	P. E. Butler	Gloucester	C 2P
Williams	3T	A. J. Morley	Bristol	
Robertson	T	J. Bayliss	Gloucester	
Batty		C. Williams	Bristol	
		P. M. Knight	Bristol	
Parkinson	2T			
Burgess				
		J. R. Gabitas	Bristol	
Colling	T	J. A. Cannon	Clifton	
Matheson		R. Cowling	Gloucester	
Urlich		J. V. Pullin	Bristol	
Murdoch		M. Burton	Gloucester	T
Macdonald		D. Watt	Bristol	
Whiting, P. J.		A. Brinn	Gloucester	
Scown		J. Watkins	Gloucester	
Kirkpatrick (capt.)		R. Hannaford	Bristol	
Sutherland		R. Smith	Gloucester	
	39 pts			12 pts

Referee: P. D'Arcy (Ireland)

What a team! That was the reaction of the crowd after the All Blacks had taken ten minutes or so to settle down and then turned on a wonderful display of fast moving, slickly rucking forwards and backs spinning the ball out along the line. A feast of 15-man rugby.

And it wasn't as if this was some soft opposition put up against them as a pipe-opener for the tour. Called Western Counties, it was in fact Gloucestershire, English county champions. Pre-match interest had been tremendous, (a) because of the Lions' first-ever victory over the All Blacks, (b) England's first-ever win against the Springboks at home, and (c) it was on the cards this strong Gloucestershire side could 'do' the tourists in their very first match. It was said that 50,000, locally and from far flung points of Britain, wanted to get to the match.

What those lucky enough to have a ticket saw was not a disappointment at false hopes raised but instead the pleasure of seeing what was clearly a great team. Which just shows how wrong first impressions can be, doesn't it?

Following the settling down period, Karam started things going with a touchline penalty (**All Blacks 3, Western Counties o**) and then Parkinson made a superb run, slicing a hole through the opposing backline, gliding past the cover defence and then, with everyone expecting him to pass to the supporting Williams, instead heading infield to score himself. Karam converted. (**9-0**) The anticipated menace of Williams came true a little later when he breezed into the Counties' 25 with no one seeming able to lay a hand on him. To make sure of the try, however, he made a crowd-pleasing toss of the ball overhead to Robertson. Karam again converted. (**15-0**)

It was heady stuff this All Black running of the ball from beautifully spun passes from Colling, the No. 2 scrum-half playing only because Going wasn't fit. Williams, to whom the tourists were obviously playing, was at it again with another scintillating run along the touchline in a movement which took play from the N.Z. 25 to just short of the Counties' line. The next try came from a well judged kick by Burgess out to Batty on the other wing and Parkinson went over from his inside pass. Karam once more converted, like Colling putting up a great show as reserve for injured No. 1 full-back Morris.

Half-time: All Blacks 21, Western Counties o

In the second half it just seemed a matter of how big a score the tourists would pile up. Williams got things going again when he fielded a poor clearance by Gabitas and hared along the touchline before passing in to Colling for a try. (**25-0**)

Belatedly the Counties exerted some pressure and were virtually presented with a try by a gentleman named Murdoch, who was to come very much into the news later in the tour. He

infringed in the line-out and when penalised had a few things to
say about it to Referee D'Arcy, who promptly awarded the
Counties a further 10 yards. This brought them right up to the
New Zealanders' line and from Cannon's tap penalty Burton
bullocked his way over. Butler converted. (**25–6**)

After this momentary interruption to their sparkling display,
the All Blacks added another try when possession from a ruck
(a foregone conclusion throughout the match) saw Williams
dash around under the posts, for Karam to convert. (**31–6**)
The Counties retaliated with a Butler penalty from lying on the
ball (**31–9**) and another from a scrum infringement. (**31–12**)

But the All Blacks finished things off with two more tries
which, since all 39 points had been scored by the tourists' backs,
sent everyone home happy in the belief that it would be a tour
of bright open rugby. First Williams scored the try of the match
when Kirkpatrick did a storming run up the middle of the field
and then, when hemmed in, tossed a huge one-handed pass out
to the winger. (**35–12**) And finally Burgess did a scything run
across field to give Williams his hat-trick.

Final Score: All Blacks 39, Western Counties 12

MATCH NO. 2

Llanelli

Stradey Park, Tuesday, October 31, 1972
Attendance: 28,000

Teams and Scorers

All Blacks		*Llanelli*	
Karam	P	R. Davies	
Williams		J. J. Williams	
Robertson		E. T. E. Bergiers	T
Hales		R. Gravelle	
		A. Hill	P
Sayers			
Burgess			
		P. Bennett	C
Colling		R. Hopkins	
Murdoch		D. B. Llewelyn	
Urlich		R. Thomas	
Whiting, G. J.		A. Crocker	
Haden		W. D. Thomas (capt.)	
Whiting, P. J.		D. L. Quinnell	
Scown		T. David	
Kirkpatrick (capt.)		G. Jenkins	
Sutherland		H. Jenkins	

Sub:
Batty for Williams

3 pts   9 pts

Referee: M. H. Titcomb (England)

There is a look that comes over the faces of the touring All
Blacks when in the course of a match it starts to become clear
that they are going to be beaten. It's not just disappointment.
It's the look of shame that they've let their country down. I
remember most vividly seeing it at Swansea in 1935 because
that was the first time I had ever seen it. After a run of 36 All
Black victories in Britain on the trot, here was this new side
going down 11–3 to Swansea. . . . And again there was that

look, on the faces of these Seventh All Blacks as Andy Hill put over a 50-yard penalty to take Llanelli into the final minutes with a lead which there seemed no chance of wresting from a team playing like demons, urged on by a crowd so fervid that for these young new tourists Stradey Park reeked of animosity.

It was Lions' coach Carwyn James, of course, who was the architect of the Llanelli triumph. Two of his most important basics: block the All Blacks at the end of the line-out, a favoured springboard for their attacks, and stop them from rucking going forward. Had not the great Colin Meads confirmed the latter: 'Successful rucking is when you're driving forward, over the gain line; it doesn't work when you have to run back to join a ruck.' The Llanelli aim, carried out with resounding success, was to stop the All Blacks in their tracks. Go out to meet them, with crushing tackles, don't wait for them to come to you.

From the kick-off the red devils tore into the attack, harried and harassed the inexperienced tourists—inexperienced as far as rugby in Welsh conditions was concerned, only one player (Kirkpatrick) having ever been exposed to it. Within two minutes the flustered All Blacks gave away a penalty, through Scown in the line-out. Bennett's kick hit the crossbar and rebounded back into play. It would have been far better for the All Blacks if it had gone over. Colling caught the ball and, pestered by onrushing Llanellians, made a hash of his clearance. Bergiers charged it down and fell gratefully on the ball as it went back over the line. Bennett converted. (**All Blacks 0, Llanelli 6**)

That six points on the board was a perfect example of the difference made to the game by the increased value for tries, to encourage going after them. In the old days the All Blacks could have overcome a 5-point lead with a couple of penalties or a penalty and a drop. Now the lead could still be gained with two scores, but one of them had to be a try. It was daunting psychologically. The All Blacks were unsettled and Llanelli intended to keep them that way.

Quinnell patrolled the line-out, joining the sea of Llanelli tacklers that swamped the end of the line at All Black throw-ins and doing great work in the front when it was Llanelli's ball. Final line-out count: 14-11 in their favour. Bennett's high kicks ahead had the tourists jittery. Sutherland recorded two of the frequent All Black knock-ons when they tried to field them. Typical of how the All Blacks were not allowed to get their machine working was Kirkpatrick, about to launch one of his now famous storming runs upfield, being dumped before he could even get under way.

In the 25th minute when Llanelli were penalised for a dummy throw-in at a line-out, Karam goaled from 40 yards. (**3–6**) But this had no effect in curbing the zest with which Llanelli were going at things, with their fanatical supporters howling for blood. They got some. Referee Titcomb had several times to halt play for warnings as fists and boots were flying.

Half-time: All Blacks 3, Llanelli 6

Llanelli having spent much of the first spell in the New Zealanders' half, it was even more so now. In the early gloom descending on the pitch one could observe Llanelli full-back Roger Davies' gear hardly muddied, as an indication of how seldom the All Blacks were able to get near his line.

With their forwards unable to make headway, the All Blacks tried to run it but midfield tacklers Roy Bergiers and Ray Gravelle allowed them none of the scope they had enjoyed at Gloucester. Burgess tried kicks ahead for his wings but twice Hales was too slow to take advantage of well directed punts that showed promise.

The Hill penalty (**3–9**) came ten minutes before the end and shortly after that Bennett showed the confidence Llanelli had in their ultimate victory by fielding another Burgess kick ahead and then proceeding to dodge out of two tackles right on his own line before putting in a beautiful kick to touch on the halfway line. And it was that which fixed the ashamed look of failure firmly on the faces of the All Blacks.

Final Score: All Blacks 3, Llanelli 9

Cardiff

Cardiff Arms Park, Saturday, November 4, 1972
Attendance: 50,000

Teams and Scorers

All Blacks		*Cardiff*	
Karam	C 2P	J. Davies	
Williams		W. Lewis	
Robertson		N. Williams	
Batty	T	A. Finlayson	
		J. Bevan	
Sayers	T		
Burgess			
		K. James	
Going		G. Edwards	T
Matheson		M. Knill	
Norton		G. Davies	
Murdoch		R. Beard	
McDonald		I. Robinson	
Whiting, P. J.		L. Baxter	
Wyllie		R. Lane	
Holmes		C. Smith	
Kirkpatrick (capt.)	T	M. John (capt.)	

Sub:
G. J. Whiting for Matheson

20 pts   4 pts

Referee: J. Young (Scotland)

The huge crowd had come to see their beloved Cardiff repeat
what Llanelli had done on the Tuesday. But these days Cardiff
is but a shadow of what they were when Cliff Morgan and
Bleddyn Williams were around and they went nowhere near
extending the tourists. The quality of the rugby was poor, at
times on the level of the sort of game you come across when
walking your dog in Regent's Park. In addition it was unruly,
the dirtiest match of the whole tour. Not merely were there

fists thrown in the forward melees. Right out in the open the
backs went after each other and more than once there was a
punch-up in progress near halfway when play had moved into
the 25. Most flagrant punch was thrown by Cardiff lock
Robinson. Matheson had followed up a high punt and as he
went in head down for the tackle on Robinson under the ball he
received a full-blooded uppercut in the face. He was carried off
on a stretcher and taken to hospital. Another blatant blow was
struck when Gareth Edwards scored Cardiff's consolation try
and Karam, unable to stop him getting over the line, was on
hand when the Cardiff scrum-half received a karate chop.
Stoppages for lectures by Scottish referee Jake Young were
frequent. It was an unpleasant match, made additionally
unsavoury by catcalls, booing and slow hand clapping from the
disgusted crowd.

In the sixth minute Karam put the All Blacks ahead with a
40-yard penalty (**All Blacks 3, Cardiff 0**) and this he repeated from the same distance four minutes later. (**6–0**) It was
the first outing of the formerly unfit Sid Going and with his
breaks and his kicks over the forwards' heads not yet working
smoothly, his efforts to impose his personality on the game
contributed to much of its scrappiness.

A minute before half-time an unsuccessful break from a line-
out by Going brought a ruck and with Batty acting as scrum-
half he sent Wyllie away on the blind side. Kirkpatrick took
over and there was no stopping him from going over near the
corner flag.

Half-time: All Blacks 10, Cardiff 0

The Matheson incident happened just after the restart,
which had featured some fierce forward exchanges. Williams by
now was being booed every time he touched the ball, the outcome of a difference of opinion he had had with Bevan.

In the 57th minute Cardiff took a quick drop-out that was so
badly executed that it went straight into the arms of Going in
midfield. With the Cardiff defence wide open in front of him a
try was on from the moment he sent Kirkpatrick away, for him
to transfer to Holmes, with Sayers finishing off the gift score.
(**14–0**)

The next from the tourists came after 68 minutes, when Batty, receiving on the left wing from Going, momentarily raised the level of the proceedings with a beautifully taken try, his first of the tour, and his hell-for-leather dash for the line was an indication of the great things that were to come from him in the following months. Karam converted. (**20–0**)

Cardiff had saved their display of expertise until right near the end, when some good passing by Roger Lane and Mervyn John on the blind side paved the way for Gareth Edwards to storm his way over. (**20–4**)

It was a not common happening, but in every way in keeping with this bad-taste-in-the-mouth match, that immediately after this try we saw John Davies teeing up on the halfway spot for a shot at goal—a penalty awarded for the karate chop on Edwards. He was not able, however, to make the try worth seven points.

Final Score: All Blacks 20, Cardiff 4

Cambridge University

Grange Road, Wednesday, November 8, 1972
Attendance: 7,000

Teams and Scorers

All Blacks		Cambridge	
Karam	C	I. S. Williamson	Sidcup GS & Fitzwillian
Batty	4T	G. P. Phillips	Gray Valley THS & Queens'
Hurst		J. M. Howard (capt.)	Birkenhead & Trinity P
Hales		N. W. Drummond	Merchiston & Fitzwillian
		R. S. Page	Haberdashers' Aske's & Emmanuel
Parkinson			
Stevens			
		C. R. Williams	Bridgend & Clare
Going (capt.)	2C	R. M. Harding	Millfield & St John's
Whiting, G. J.		G. Rees	Neath GS & Emmanuel
Urlich		J. M. Smith	Neath GS & Selwyn
Lambert		G. P. Goodall	Sherborne & St Catherine's
Haden		G. R. Thomas	Llandello GS & Christ's
Eliason		R. M. Wilkinson	St Albans & Emmanuel
Wyllie	T	A. D. Foley	Fettes & Christ's
Sutherland	2T	J. P. Dickins	Oundle & Corpus Christi
Stewart		W. A. Jones	Campbell Coll, Belfast & Queens
Sub:		*Subs:*	
Scown for Sutherland		T. Lintott	Blundell's & Christ's
		A. Walker	Luton GS & Emmanuel
34 pts			3 pts

Referee: G. Domercq (France)

Cambridge was the first piece of cake on the All Blacks' fixture menu but the varsity lads were determined to stop them making a feast of it. Despite the lopsided look of the scoreline it was not an impressive win, especially when one bears in mind that for much of the time Cambridge played with fourteen men, having used up both their substitutes. The All Black forwards did not dominate. The best forward on the day was 21-year-old Cambridge lock Bob Wilkinson, at once acknowledged as a man with a future by both the onlookers and the New Zealanders. Much of the tourists' play was untidy, due in no small measure to his activities at the line-out and in the loose. Going, keen to leave his mark on the match, attempted much but was messy in a good deal of his work. Stevens suffered by his bad service. The All Blacks could be thankful that Grant Batty was in cracking form, to boost the total with his four tries.

Much of the scoring was done when Cambridge had men off the field and were waiting for their replacements. The All Blacks had gone into the lead with an unconverted try in the 26th minute (**All Blacks 4, Cambridge 0**) but ten minutes later prop Charlie Goodall had to retire with a cheekbone fracture and before substitute Tim Lintott could get on, Batty had streaked over for another.

Half-time: All Blacks 8, Cambridge 0

Eight minutes after the interval Cambridge lost their full-back, Ian Williamson, with a fractured thumb, and Batty took advantage of his absence to go over for his third try. (**12–0**) Karam was having no luck with his conversions. In fact it was to be his worst kicking day of the tour, with a total of seven misses before Going took over his duties.

Cambridge's second substitute, Adrian Walker, had just come on when it seemed to be turning into a shuttle service of injured players and replacements as lock Richard Thomas now had to go off for three minutes for attention to a cut face. Again the All Blacks took advantage of their 14-man opposition, when Sutherland bullocked his way over. (**16–0**)

Following a penalty by John Howard (**16–3**), Thomas had returned to the field when Sutherland again used his weight to score 20 minutes from the end and this time Karam had his sole successful shot at goal. (**22–3**) But eight minutes afterwards Cambridge centre Norman Drummond had to go off with a fractured thumb and from then on they had no option but to continue with a man short, their replacement quota having been used up.

It was to their credit that the All Blacks did not run wild, as might have been expected. They were restricted to but two more tries—Batty's fourth, converted by Going (**28–3**) and one by Wyllie, also converted by Going.

Final Score: All Blacks 34, Cambridge 3

MATCH NO. 5

London Counties

Twickenham, Saturday, November 11, 1972
Attendance: 35,000

Teams and Scorers

All Blacks			London Counties	
Karam	2C T		A. M. Jorden	Blackheath & Eastern Counties P
Williams	T		A. Richards	London Welsh & Surrey
Hurst	T		S. J. Dawes	London Welsh & Middlesex
Batty	T		D. A. Cooke	Harlequins & Kent
			M. P. Bulpitt	Blackheath & Eastern Counties
Parkingson				
Burgess				
			C. D. Saville	Blackheath & Surrey
Going			W. G. Hullin	London Welsh & Surrey
Matheson			R. L. Barlow	Rosslyn Park & Middlesex
Norton			A. V. Boddy	Met Police & Middlesex
Murdoch			R. L. Challis	London Scottish & Kent
Macdonald			C. W. Ralston	Richmond & Middlesex
Whiting, P. J.			M. G. Molloy	London Irish & Surrey
Stewart			A. L. Bucknall (capt.)	Richmond & Eastern Counties
Kirkpatrick (capt.)			S. James	London Welsh & Surrey
Sutherland	T		A. G. Ripley	Rosslyn Park & Middlesex

Sub:
Sayers for Hurst

24 pts   3 pts

Referee: G. A. Jameson (Ireland)

After an unsatisfactory mixed bag in their first four matches (bright opening at Gloucester, defeat at Llanelli, unpleasantness at Cardiff and unimpressive win against weak opposition at

Cambridge) it was felt that it was up to the All Blacks to put things right with a good display at the Twickenham 'shop window'. They didn't. There was one glorious end-to-end try reminiscent of a similar thriller by Whineray's men in the equivalent fixture but this isolated ray of sunshine was hardly one's money's worth at today's prices.

It wasn't as if London Counties kept them in check. They had all the possession in the world (23–14 line-outs, five tight heads, rucked ball at will) and what possession London did get was usually wasted by appalling handling by their halves, Hullin and Saville, always harassed. So the stage was set for a great show by the tourists. That it didn't come (apart from that try) was put down by observers to a poor All Black backline. In truth, however, the heavy hand of Sid Going was on the match. For the main part he played it close to the pack, as though it was a closely fought Test, instead of freely distributing all that good ball to the waiting backs once it was established which was undoubtedly the better side.

On a bitterly cold, windswept day there was indecisive play for the first quarter but then the slick rucking of the All Blacks brought its inevitable try as Sutherland picked up and dabbed the ball over the line. (**All Blacks 4, London Counties 0**) A crooked put-in by Going gave Jorden the chance to goal from 30 yards (**4–3**) but the home side never really threatened to do much more in the way of scoring.

Karam pulled off a crafty move in the 34th minute when one of the Londoners was injured. A penalty had been awarded in their 25 and when the injury was being attended to the touch judges went around to the posts, anticipating a Karam shot at goal. Karam, however, hadn't indicated he was going to take a shot, so technically he was within his rights when he took a tap penalty and caught the opposition unawares as he dashed for the line. (**8–3**)

The showpiece of the match came just on half-time. At a maul barely a dozen yards from the All Black line Going got possession and having shrugged off some tacklers gave to Kirkpatrick. He stormed up the middle and what the French call the Black Tide started to flow as Stewart, Macdonald, Burgess and Parkinson handled before Hurst was put over near the corner for what was probably their best team try scored on the tour.

Half-time: All Blacks 12, London Counties 3

Anyone who thought that that gem would be the prelude to a flood of really sparkling stuff from the tourists in the second spell was away out in his thinking. We did have a beautifully judged kick by Burgess for a Williams try, converted by Karam (**18–3**), but then the game became so scrappy and was of such monumental dullness that when the man next to me had a nosebleed I welcomed something to bring interest to.

It was not until right on time that we got what one felt we should have been having constantly. Going whipped the ball out from a line-out and it sped along the All Black backline in copybook style for Batty to round it off with a flourish and Karam to add the extra points. (**24–3**) This try prompted Vivian Jenkins in the *Sunday Times* next day to call the shot very accurately: 'Batty at the moment looks even more dangerous than the famed Bryan Williams on the right wing. With his jack-rabbit running this sturdily built 5 ft 5½ ins player looks like becoming one of the "hit" players of the tour.'

Final Score: All Blacks 24, London Counties 3

MATCH NO. 6

Leinster

Lansdowne Road, Dublin, Wednesday, November 15, 1972
Attendance: 25,000

Teams and Scorers

All Blacks		Leinster		
Going (capt.)	C	A. H. Ensor	Wanderers	C P
Williams	P	T. Grace	St. Mary's	
Hales		K. Flynn	Wanderers	
Skudder	T	P. Andruchetti	St. Mary's	
		A. T. A. Duggan	Lansdowne	
Sayers				
Stevens				
		M. Quinn	Lansdowne	
Colling		J. Moloney	St. Mary's	
Whiting, G. J.		J. F. Lynch (capt.)	St. Mary's	
Urlich		D. O. Barry	Wanderers	
Lambert		N. Dwyer	Lansdowne	
Whiting, P. J.	T	K. Mays	UCD	
Eliason		C. F. P. Feighery	Lansdowne	
Wyllie	T	J. Craig	Lansdowne	
Holmes		J. F. Slattery	Blackrock	
Scown		W. Duggan	Blackrock	T

Sub:
P. Inglis (Lansdowne) for Slattery

17 pts   9 pts

Referee: M. Joseph (Wales)

The comment was made that if an uninformed observer had dropped in on the match he might have been forgiven for thinking that it was Leinster which was the international touring side. They rucked like All Blacks in the best tradition and went at things with such zest and determination that with less than ten minutes to go they were leading 9–7 and looked right to bring about an historic upset. It was only two errors in those last stages that enabled the All Blacks to emerge fortunate winners.

With Morris not yet fit and Karam in need of a rest, Going had taken the field as full-back and as captain, Kirkpatrick also resting. A heavily bandaged Skudder having his first outing and winger Hales at centre, the All Blacks were very much of a makeshift midweek side. But it would be unfair to use this to detract from a great showing by Leinster.

The goal-kicking chores were shared by Williams and Going and even despite the stiff breeze in their favour it was not until the fourth penalty that Williams was able to coax one over from 30 yards, for the only score in the first spell.

Half-time: All Blacks 3, Leinster 0

Ensor having equalised in the fourth minute of the second half (**3–3**), the crowd erupted when a good move by Leinster saw Moloney get possession from a five-yard scrum for Quinn to do the loop with Andruchetti and then send Grace over by the right corner flag. But fortunately for the All Blacks Quinn's final pass had been forward.

Having been under considerable pressure from the ferocity of the Irish approach, the tourists managed to push them back and there was a succession of no fewer than six five-yard scrums on the Leinster line. It was too much to ask that such sterling defence could hold out indefinitely and at the last Colling went on the blind side to put Wyllie over. (**7–3**)

But back came Leinster, with an attack from their own 25 which featured Moloney, Quinn and Ensor, the ball finally reaching Grace, whose kick ahead perversely veered away from the line and into touch ten yards out. The All Blacks' long throw-in was tapped away from their end men and Bill Duggan gratefully latched on to it to bring the scores level. The hushed silence as Ensor ran up for the kick exploded into yells of delight as the conversion went over and Leinster had snatched the lead. (**7–9**)

But sadly for the wildly enthusiastic crowd the All Blacks were let off the hook. Error number one came when both Leinster wings, Grace and Al Duggan, went to retrieve a Colling kick into their 25 and got entangled with each other.

Sayers moved in to scoop up the ball and pass out to Skudder for a try. (**11–9**) All was not lost but with just six minutes to go error number two let the All Blacks hoist themselves out of reach. A misdirected kick by Quinn was fielded by Going, who sent up a huge one in return. Ensor made a sad hash of fielding it and Peter Whiting, following up at full tilt, had the ball bounce neatly into his hands, to sail over for a try, which Going converted.

Final Score: All Blacks 17, Leinster 9

Ulster

Ravenhill Park, Belfast, Saturday, November 18, 1972
Attendance: 20,000

Teams and Scorers

All Blacks		Ulster		
Karam	C 3P	B. D. E. Marshall	CIYMS	C
Williams		J. Miles	Malone	
Hales	T	R. A. Millikin	Bangor	
Batty		A. Goodrich	Queen's U	
		C. H. McKibbin	Instonians	
Sayers				
Burgess	T			
.		A. Harrison	Collegians	
Going		W. R. Oakes	Instonians	
Matheson		P. J. Agnew	CIYMS	
Urlich		K. W. Kennedy	London Irish	
Murdoch		R. J. Clegg	Bangor	
Macdonald		W. J. McBride (capt.)	Ballymena	
Haden		C. W. Murtagh	Portadown	
Kirkpatrick (capt.)		J. C. Davidson	Dungannon	
Wyllie		H. W. Steele	Queen's U	T
Stewart		S. A. McKinney	Dungannon	
Sub:				
Skudder for Williams				
	19 pts			6 pts

Referee: R. F. Johnson (England)

The All Blacks made a great hit merely by running on to the field. Because of the troubles there has been an avoidance of Belfast by sports teams. The locals showed their appreciation of the New Zealanders not letting such things stand in the way of their visit, with an ovation as they came on to play, plus another when the game was over. In some measure this improved the All Black image, becoming somewhat tarnished elsewhere in the British Isles.

The main resistance from Ulster came, as expected, from

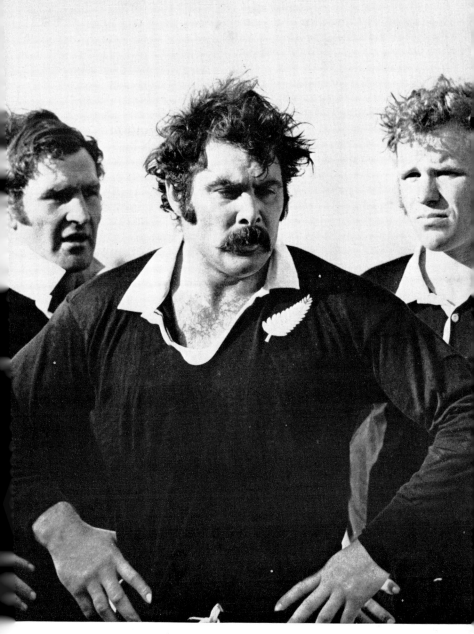

NOT WANTED ON THE VOYAGE
Keith Murdoch

SID GOING, master of 9-man rugby, in a typically happy situation among his forwards, against North Eastern Counties.

GOING AND KIRKPATRICK: KEY MEN OF THE SIDE

(*At left*) they link, while the All Blacks' backs languish in the rear.

(*Opposite*) White of Midland Counties (West) fails to stop Kirkpatrick as he sets off on one of his characteristic runs that were such a feature of the tour.

KIRKPATRICK'S BACK-ROW RUNNING MATES

Flanker Alex Wyllie (*above* handing on after being tackled by England's Ripley) and No. 8 Alan Sutherland (*below* scoring against London Counties) combined with Kirkpatrick to almost, but not quite, rise to the heights scaled by Waka Nathan, Tremain and Lochore.

their forwards, drilled by Ireland and Lions veteran Willie John McBride. The backs, however, suffered from the absence of Mike Gibson, out through a back injury, and showed little penetration, which counted very much against them in the first half in particular when the strong wind gave them territorial advantage.

Key to the All Blacks' win was as Kirkpatrick put it afterwards: 'We took our chances and most of all we kicked our penalty goals.' Karam had a good day and kicked the first of his three penalties in the first half (**All Blacks 3, Ulster 0**), when the tourists were very much restricted to sallies into Ulster ground. During one such foray Burgess charged down a clearing kick by his opposite number and when the ball bounced back over the line under the posts merely had to run in and touch down. Karam's conversion was a formality.

Half-time: All Blacks 9, Ulster 0

Just how useful the wind was we saw when Karam, not normally a 'siege gun' kicker, put over a soaring 56-yarder (**12–0**) and after he had kicked another penalty (**15–0**), the All Blacks produced the best movement of the match. For once their midfield backs used some ingenuity and Going and Sayers worked a perfect scissors which put Hales through for a try. (**19–0**)

However, despite those daunting 19 points the Ulster forwards were still determined to make a battle of it and after a succession of fiery rucks they managed to work play to within striking distance of the New Zealanders' line. There, far out on the right, their No. 8, Steele, got possession following another ruck and hurled himself over. Marshall put over a superb conversion from right on the touchline.

Final Score: All Blacks 19, Ulster 6

North West Counties

Workington, Cumberland, Wednesday, November 22, 1972
Attendance: 12,000

Teams and Scorers

All Blacks		*North West Countries*		
Morris	2P	B. J. O'Driscoll	Manchester	
Skudder	T	A. A. Richards	Flyde	
Hales		C. S. Wardlow	Coventry	D
Batty	T	D. F. K. Roughley	Liverpool	
		P. S. Maxwell	Richmond	2T
Sayers				
Burgess		A. R. Cowman	Coventry	C P
Colling		S. Smith	Sale	
Lambert		W. F. Anderson	Orrell	
Norton		J. Lansbury	Sale	
Whiting, G. J.		F. E. Cotton (c̀apt.)	Loughborough Cols	
Whiting, P. J.		A. R. Trickey	Sale	
Eliason		M. M. Leadbetter	Broughton Park	
Kirkpatrick (capt.)		D. Robinson	Gosforth	
Sutherland		P. J. Dixon	Gosforth	
Holmes		A. Neary	Broughton Park	
Sub:				
Going for Colling				
14 pts				16 pts

Referee: T. F. E. Grierson (Scotland)

The North West took on the All Blacks at their own game and beat them. Slick rucking was the cornerstone of their success and a perfect example of the difference that coaching can make, since this could hardly be called a hotbed of rugby with a tradition of being troublesome to tourists. In fact many of the boys who swarmed on to the pitch in this isolated Cumberland steel town were perhaps present at the first rugby match they had ever seen—what else is there to do in Workington on a Wednesday afternoon? And what an historic match these neo-

phytes had chosen—the first time any team in England outside
the national side had ever beaten the All Blacks, after 86
attempts in 67 years of trying.

It was a triumph for discarded England coach John Burgess,
who said: 'We beat them with heart and with courage. We out-
thought them, confused them and mesmerised them to prove
that England has the players to shatter the myth of this in-
vincible New Zealand power. The All Blacks are not ogres.
They came here for a soft touch. We showed them that English
rugby isn't a soft touch any more.'

Mentally and physically prepared by Burgess, the North-
Westerners not only outdid the tourists in the power rugby up
front but also behind the pack they had the courage to be
adventurous and the confidence that bold back play would pay
dividends against the less strong department of this touring side.

Morris, making his debut in Britain, began most unhappily.
In their eagerness to harass the All Blacks from the outset the
North West gave away three kickable penalties in the first two
minutes, all of which Morris missed. But he at last clicked with
another in the fourth minute. (**All Blacks 3, North West
Counties o**) The Counties put the pressure on and from a line-
out near the All Black line when scrum-half Steve Smith
whipped the ball to Wardlow he was so in the clear that he had
all the time in the world to make sure of his dropped goal. (**3–3**)

The first try of the match was entirely of Burgess's making.
When the ball came to him from Sutherland standing off from a
scrum he made a great break on the blind side before giving to
Batty to complete the move. (**7–3**) To which North West
promptly responded with their first try, equally well taken.
From a line-out Anderson forged his way through and from a
ruck Roughley's long pass missed out co-centre Wardlow, for
Maxwell to streak over. The applause was tumultuous as
Cowman's conversion attempt from touch went over and the
Counties were in the lead. (**7–9**)

A handy lead to turn round with, but things went a bit quiet
crowdwise when Morris managed another penalty just before
the break.

Half-time: All Blacks 10, North West Counties 9

Cheated of their lead, the North West seemed unlikely to get it again during the early part of the second spell, the All Blacks now having apparently settled down after their half-time team-talk. They consolidated their position when a high kick by Burgess brought an O'Driscoll fumble. Skudder picked up and fended off both Smith and Richards in his progress to the line. (**14–9**)

But now came the great comeback by the home side. First of their two vital scores was something of a present. The tendency of Batty to delay his throw at line-outs now proved disastrous. Referee Grierson invoked Law 34 (Waste of time caused intentionally by a player) against him and Cowman goaled the penalty. (**14–12**)

The final, match-winning score, however, was no such gift. It was a brilliant bit of play well worthy of the ecstatic storming on to the pitch that followed it. From a line-out on the right Neary's tapdown was taken by Cotton, who passed to Cowman, heading straight for the posts. The All Black defence looked as though it would survive. So much so that Cowman couldn't get in a normal pass but had to toss it high over the defenders to Wardlow. And Wardlow then entered his name in the local book of heroes by not catching it but instead executing a beautifully judged tap-on to winger Maxwell, the speed at which it reached him giving him an overlap to the line.

Final Score: All Blacks 14, North West Counties 16

Rest of Scottish Districts

Mansfield Park, Hawick, Saturday, November 25, 1972
Attendance: 15,000

Teams and Scorers

All Blacks		Rest of Scottish Districts		
Karam	2C 2P	A. Brown	Gala	
Williams		W. C. C. Steele	Bedford	
Hales	T	I. N. M. Frame	Gala	
Skudder	T	J. B. Renwick	Hawick	
		L. G. Dick	Loughborough Cols	
Parkinson	T			
Stevens				
		R. I. McGreechan	Headingley	
Going	T	I. G. McCrae	Gordonians	
Murdoch		N. Suddon	Hawick	
Norton		F. A. L. Laidlaw	Melrose	
Matheson		R. D. H. Bryce	Bristol	
Whiting, P. J.		A. R. McHarg	London Scottish	
Macdonald		P. K. Stagg	Sale	
Kirkpatrick (capt.)		N. A. McEwan	Gala	
Wyllie		W. Lauder	Neath	
Scown		P. C. Brown (capt.)	Gala	2P
		Subs:		
		J. Henderson (Melrose) for McCrae		
		D. Aitchison (Highland) for A. Brown		
	26 pts			**6 pts**

Referee: J. Kelleher (Wales)

As they drove from their hotel in Peebles through the delightful Border country for their match at Hawick, the All Blacks knew they just had to win this one. To add a third defeat to their record would have made it equal to the worst the 1935 All Blacks had done with only a third of the tour gone. And on their side of the fence the Scots in this dedicated stronghold of rugby knew they were there for the taking and were out to chalk up the first ever Scottish victory against them.

In the event, however, after a comparatively even first half
the All Blacks had a period of sustained dominance in which
they ran in three tries, forwards and backs playing like a well-
oiled machine. It was beautiful rugby to watch, only for the
tourists to revert in the final quarter of an hour to the sort of
stuff that brought them the nickname of the All Greys. Another
of the uneven performances of a side lacking confidence.

Peter Brown, nose-wiping, nonchalant place-kicker, idol of
the Borders, lived right up to his reputation with a penalty
from a crooked Going put-in just three minutes from the start.
(All Blacks 0, Scottish Districts 3) Karam equalised from a
Districts' scrum infringement **(3–3)** and then gave the tourists
the lead with another of the same order **(6–3)**. The Crooked
Going Put-in, which was to become such a feature of this tour,
was in evidence again, to enable Peter Brown to bring the
Districts back to parity. **(6–6)**

It wasn't until ten minutes before the break that the All
Blacks gave an indication of more constructive rugby to come.
They worked their way to within striking distance of the
Districts' line and at a scrum, although the locals won the heel
the pass back to Arthur Brown for a safety kick was fumbled.
The All Black forwards rucked slickly, Going getting the ball so
promptly that he had time to debate whether to use the open or
blind side, before eventually deciding on the latter and putting
Skudder over.

Half-time: All Blacks 10, Scottish Districts 6

Stevens started off the All Black session of good co-ordinated
rugby when he dummied through and drew the defence so
effectively that as he transferred to Hales there were three men
outside him in support not needed as he crossed the line. **(14–6)**
The tourists at once came back for more and again rucking with
precision presented Going with the ball with nothing to do but
drop over for a try, converted by Karam. **(20–6)**
Parkinson then gave a display of the brilliance that was
expected of him but which unfortunately he was to produce but
rarely on the tour. With a great solo effort he weaved his way
through an assembly of tacklers as the tourists were now plainly
in command. **(26–6)** But the pile-up of points from them which

one would have thought would have been logical in the final stages never came. It was the home side which was to do all the bright things at the end, tossing the ball about as if they were playing Sevens—the game which had been invented just up the road at Melrose. But they seemed to be so fascinated by inter-passing that they omitted to remember that the object of the operation was to get the ball across the line.

Final Score: All Blacks 26, Scottish Districts 6

Gwent

Welfare Sports Ground, Ebbw Vale,
Tuesday, November 28, 1972
Attendance: 18,000

Teams and Scorers

All Blacks		Gwent		
Morris	C P D	R. Pugh	Pontypool	P
Hales		A. Browning	Newbridge	
Parkinson		J. Taylor	Pontypool	
Batty		R. Duggan	Bedwas	
		R. Parry	Ebbw Vale	
Sayers				
Stevens	T			
		M. Grindle	Ebbw Vale	
Going		G. Turner	Ebbw Vale	T
Whiting, G. J.		G. Howls	Ebbw Vale	
Urlich		A. Williams	Newbridge	
Murdoch		A. Faulkner	Pontypool	
Whiting, P. J.		R. Bendall	Newbridge	
Haden	T	S. Geary	Newbridge	
Kirkpatrick (capt.)		G. Evans	Ebbw Vale	
Sutherland		D. Hughes (capt.)	Newbridge	
Stewart		T. Cobner	Pontypool	
Sub:		*Sub:*		
Scown for Batty		A. Tucker (Blaina) for Evans		
	16 pts			7 pts

Referee: K. Pattinson (England)

For their third Welsh fixture the All Blacks were in the land of
the giant killers. Had not Gwent scored a sensational victory
over the 1969 Springboks, thoroughly deserved on a day when
the South Africans were not distracted by demonstrators? But
this time they came nowhere near a repeat. The All Blacks beat
them convincingly, even if, with such dominance as a 23–5
count at the rucks, one would have expected their superiority to
show more clearly in the scoreline. But Going was playing and

of course that held the score down. Tries stemming directly from action in and around the pack cannot be produced so quickly and in such numbers as when the ball is whipped out consistently to the backs, as by Colling.

The All Blacks' opening score came six minutes from the start when a 35-yard penalty attempt by Morris hit a post and rebounded to Cobner, who failed to gather it. Haden, who was to be more and more prominent in the loose as the tour progressed, was quick on the follow-up and was there to snap it up and score, Morris converting. (**All Blacks 6, Gwent 0**) Batty had to leave the field limping after some lively runs and we had the unusual sight of Scown on the wing, although he had been seen in action there in his native Taranaki.

Gwent could have ended the first spell on level terms but two not very difficult shots at goal by Pugh went astray.

Half-time: All Blacks 6, Gwent 0

Morris increased the lead immediately after the restart with a 35-yard penalty (**9–0**) and then lived right up to his pre-tour publicity with a magnificent dropped goal from 40 yards out which seemed still to be gaining height as it went over the bar. (**12–0**) Done by the expert Morris is in this department it was only a pity that his few appearances on tour meant that there weren't many of these to be seen. He contributed two to a mere four throughout the tour.

Pugh responded with a penalty (**12–3**) but then the All Blacks started to click with some sort of rhythm, several good movements being frustrated only by stout Gwent tackling. But at length they got through for their second try, started by Going from a tap penalty in midfield and completed by a great 30-yard sprint by Stevens. (**16–3**)

Gwent's consolation try came from a strike against the head on the All Black line and a blind-side dash by Turner.

Final Score: All Blacks 16, Gwent 7

Wales

Cardiff Arms Park, Saturday, December 2, 1972
Attendance: 55,000

Teams and Scorers

New Zealand		Wales		
†Karam	5P	J. P. R. Williams	London Welsh	
Williams		T. G. R. Davies	London Welsh	
Hales		R. T. E. Bergiers	Llanelli	
†Batty		J. L. Shanklin	London Welsh	
		J. C. Bevan	Cardiff	
Parkinson				
Burgess				
		P. Bennett	Llanelli	4P
Going		G. O. Edwards	Cardiff	
Matheson		†G. Shaw	Neath	
Norton		J. Young	London Welsh	
Murdoch	T	D. B. Llewelyn	Llanelli	
†Macdonald		W. D. Thomas (capt.)	Llanelli	
Whiting, P. J.		D. L. Quinnell	Llanelli	
Wyllie		W. D. Morris	Neath	
Sutherland		T. M. Davies	Swansea	
Kirkpatrick (capt.)		J. Taylor	London Welsh	
Sub :				
Scown for Wyllie				
19 pts				16 pts

Referee: R. F. Johnson (England)   †New cap

This was a Test which Wales should be ashamed at not winning. On paper there was no other logical result. They were vastly more experienced in big-time rugby, an assembly of no fewer than 227 Welsh and Lions caps against a piddling 83 of the young New Zealand side. They had the confidence of being International Champions, compared to the All Blacks' non-confidence of two defeats in their first ten matches, worst record of any visiting New Zealand side in history. And, highly important, Wales were playing at home before the Arms Park crowd famous for urging them on and notorious for intimidating visitors.

The moaning at the bar by Welsh supporters afterwards was unjustified, since with all those cards stacked in their side's favour they should have done better than merely managing to come near to drawing the match in injury time.

The game was divided precisely into two parts: the first half all New Zealand and the second all Wales. With the reputation in recent years of being 'a second-half team', this time Wales didn't have enough guns in the end to bring them through. Which was almost literally true, in view of the fact that it was shots at goal that really decided it. Karam landed five of his six penalties; Bennett put over but four of his seven. In an article in John Reason's new book, *The Lions Speak*, Barry John elevates round-the-corner kicking to an art. As executed by Phil Bennett it is not.

The match was but two minutes old when New Zealand were presented with a penalty which gave them just the sort of confidence they lacked when they took the field. At a scrum in front of the Welsh posts Morris unwisely went around to molest Going before the ball was out and Karam gratefully goaled. **(New Zealand 3, Wales 0)** Seven minutes later Welsh hooker Jeff Young, not nicknamed 'Twitchy Feet' without good reason, gave away the first of three penalties also gratefully accepted by Karam. **(6–0)**

With that useful lead on the board so early, the All Blacks went at things with a show of assurance, even if the numerous attacks they mounted were methodical rather than colourful. Their advances were made mainly through Going playing it tight to the pack and when he did release it to the backs it invariably got no further than Burgess. Thirty-five minutes in fact elapsed before their first sending of the ball out to a wing by hand. Burgess used the high punt ahead so favoured by this team and a sound enough tactic this day when morning rain meant sodden turf. Better to let the Welsh do the fumbling than risk back movements and dropped balls against a back division renowned as opportunists.

For their part, Wales were equally unadventurous and were to regret the fact that when they did move the ball about and indicate that they were clearly superior before it was too late.

The solitary New Zealand try came when Going kicked over his forwards' heads along the touchline and was himself first on the scene when Bevan had trouble with the bounce. With the surge of forwards following up it was Murdoch who got the touchdown in the rough-and-tumble on the line. (**10–0**)

In the twenty-fourth minute Bennett, having missed one penalty, now goaled when New Zealand infringed at a ruck (**10–3**) but Karam immediately discounted it with his third successive penalty when hooker Young erred again.

Half-time: New Zealand 13, Wales 3

It was interesting that that 13–3 was exactly the same deficit that had faced Wales at half-time in their match against England two years before when, seemingly a beaten team, they had magnificently made a victory of it. And now this half was not far gone before they looked as though they were going to do a repeat.

What sparked them off was a great Bevan try. It had its beginnings at a midfield scrum near halfway when Going got possession against the put-in. With his backs outside him all ready to go he decided instead to do one of his famous solo breaks, and was nailed. The ball was kicked into the New Zealand half and bounced up handily for Bennett, who tossed a long one out to Bevan on the left wing. He shrugged off first Hales and then Karam in a marvellous dash for the corner. (**13–7**)

This was just four minutes after the restart and the crowd having greeted it with a tumult that would have made earplugs useful, were screaming again when three minutes later Bennett brought Wales within three points of the tourists with a penalty. (**13–10**)

This lifted the Welshmen. They were going like a bomb now and even Karam's fourth penalty (**16–10**) didn't seem to worry them unduly. They were moving the ball so smoothly that the ones who were worried were the All Blacks. They seemed to have no answer but obstruction and late tackles. From one such tackle Bennett put over another penalty (**16–13**) and shortly afterwards the lead seemed to be theirs when John Williams, after a subdued first half but now joining the other backs in attack with his customary flair, touched down near the posts. But there were no real complaints from the crowd when referee Johnson ruled against it for rabbitting.

Karam's fifth penalty (**19–13**) was something of a setback but with Wales completely dominating the play it seemed just a matter of time before they would come out on top. New Zealand, somewhat desperate, again obstructed and Bennett kicked the goal. (**19–16**)

With a matter of minutes to go it was all Wales' pressure and it seemed for New Zealand that nothing but the clock could save them. Through into injury time Wales fought like demons to get the try necessary for victory. Then with the final whistle imminent John Williams kicked upfield and started to follow up. The referee ruled obstruction against the men who got in his way and Bennett, with a 40-yard penalty, had the chance at least to get a draw for Wales, but he just wasn't able to pull it off.

Final Score: New Zealand 19, Wales 16

Midland Counties (West)

Moseley, Birmingham, Wednesday, December 6, 1972
Attendance: 14,000

Teams and Scorers

All Blacks		Midland Counties (West)		
Morris		S. J. Doble	Moseley	C P
Williams		D. J. Duckham (capt.)	Coventry	T
Hurst	T	P. S. Preece	Coventry	
Skudder		M. K. Swain	Moseley	
		M. J. Cooper	Moseley	T
Sayers	T			
Burgess				
		J. F. Finlan	Moseley	D
Colling		J. G. Webster	Moseley	
Lambert		T. F. Corless	Birmingham	
Urlich		J. D. Gray	Coventry	
Whiting, G. J.		K. E. Fairbrother	Coventry	
Haden		N. E. Horton	Moseley	
Eliason		L. Smith	Moseley	
Stewart		I. N. Pringle	Moseley	
Holmes		J. C. White	Moseley	
Kirkpatrick (capt.)		T. M. Cowell	Rugby	
	8 pts			16 pts

Referee: R. Lewis

Ernie Todd's almost unbelievable statement at the outset of the
tour that the All Blacks were not going to study the opposition
in the selection of their teams seemed to be very much borne out
in this match. West Midlands were certainly no midweek soft
touch—the forwards in this area are always known to be
formidable and this day they had behind them no fewer than
five of England's current line-up of backs. Yet into the field the
tourists put all their Skudder-types, bolstered by only three,
two backs and a forward, of their current Test side. They were
inviting disaster, which duly materialised.

As at Llanelli they were thrown out of kilter right at the

beginning—but even more so. As late-comers were still settling into their seats Midlands won the first two line-outs and from the second Finlan dropped a goal. (**All Blacks o, West Midlands 3**) They won the first scrum, against the head, for Webster to dash off on the open side and send along the line for Cooper to score. (**o–7**) When the All Blacks won one against the put-in Pringle kicked the ball out of Colling's hands, Sayers made a mess of the clearance and slick passing by Horton, Corless, Cowell, Finlan and Preece put big Duckham around the flank of the disorganised defence. Doble converted (**o–13**) and in the space of just eight minutes the Midlands had further demoralised a side already at a low ebb following the sending home of Keith Murdoch two days before.

More than 20 minutes had passed before they managed to show any fight-back. They reached the Midlands' 25 for the first time, first Holmes and then Kirkpatrick and Burgess relieving the pressure with good individual runs. In a Midlands' back movement Swain gave Preece a pass with Hurst right on top of him and Sayers was able to pick up the loose ball for a try. (**4–13**) But just before half-time Doble with a penalty put the All Blacks back in that daunting position of having to score three times to win.

Half-time: All Blacks 4, West Midlands 16

And in the second half they could manage only one of the three required scores. Having in the first spell lived up to Scottish coach Jim Greenwood's demand to keep pressuring the All Blacks into mistakes, the Midlands never let up. They came down particularly hard on Colling, who was never allowed to set up any sort of rhythm among the backs.

In the 23rd minute Kirkpatrick, fighting desperately to prevent his side being linked in the record books with the 1935 All Blacks and their worst ever three defeats, battled through from a maul and after being joined by Graham Whiting and Holmes the move was finished off by Hurst. (**8–16**) Morris's failure to convert was disheartening. Having missed the other conversion and failed with four kickable penalties, Morris was sadly unable to give his team the sort of lift they needed from kicked points on the board. It was, in fact, to be the only match of the tour in which no All Black points had come from the boot.

Despairing of poor Morris, Kirkpatrick henceforth ran each and every penalty. It all had the look of desperation about it and with the Midlands crowd going crazy the All Blacks looked and were a thoroughly beaten side.

Final Score: All Blacks 8, West Midlands 16

North East Counties

Lidget Green, Bradford, Saturday, December 9, 1972
Attendance: 14,000

Teams and Scorers

All Blacks		North East Counties		
Karam	C	B. Patrick	Gosforth	
Williams		D. W. Carr	Gosforth	
Hurst		I. R. McGeechan	Headingley	
Batty	T	P. S. Warfield	Durham U	
		A. Cheshire	Harrogate	
Parkinson				
Stevens				
		A. G. B. Old	Leicester	P
Going	D	M. Young	Gosforth	
Matheson		C. White	Northern	
Norton		D. F. Madsen	Gosforth	
Whiting, G. J.		P. McLoughlin	Northern	
Haden		R. M. Uttley	Gosforth	
Whiting, P. J.		J. Hall	Cheltenham	
Scown		R. J. Leathley	Halifax	
Kirkpatrick (capt.)		T. Donovan	Headingley	
Sutherland		P. G. Nash	Middlesbrough	
Sub:				
Skudder for Batty				
	9 pts			3 pts

Referee: F. Palmade (France)

In contrast to the B team they had put out against strong
West Midlands on the Wednesday, the All Blacks now fielded
ten of their Wales' Test side—against opposition which contained but a solitary International, Alan Old. But perhaps it
was as well that they had fielded an experienced side. On a cold
day of drizzling rain the North Easterners unexpectedly put
up a great fight. Their defence was notable, especially from
centre Peter Warfield, protege of crash tackler Danny Hearn,
the back row of Leathley, Donovan and Nash, and 18-year-old

full-back Brian Patrick who as well as his superb saving tackles fielded the slippery ball magnificently and time and again earned applause for his touch-finding.

For some reason hard to fathom, perhaps to improve their image, the All Blacks started by trying to run the ball. But dropped passes soon persuaded them to abandon that and return to the safer formula, for conditions like this, of their more familiar forward game. However, it was symbolic of the general improvement of British rugby that their forwards could not swamp this non-rated local side.

The opening score, in fact, was not theirs. In the 23rd minute Old put over a penalty (**All Blacks 0, North East Counties 3**) and it was not until nine minutes into the second quarter that the All Blacks could take the lead. Stevens, receiving from a ruck, made a half break and then Hurst, with Parkinson and Batty outside him, shot the ball straight out to the winger, who brilliantly beat two defenders to go over near the corner. Karam oddly enough managed this shot at goal (**6–3**), while missing five easier penalties, to what must have been chagrin to any Welshman present.

Half-time: All Blacks 6, North East Counties 3

As conditions got progressively worse it was impossible for there to be much in the way of cohesive play, even though the game was still very much alive for the locals with the tourists only three points ahead.

Going, however, brightened the muddied proceedings with a flash of genius which was to make things safe for the All Blacks. Not famed as a drop-kicker—how many scrum-halves are?—he suddenly produced one that will always be remembered by those who saw it. Getting the ball in a melee more than 30 yards out from the posts and seemingly hemmed in by team-mates and opponents he hoisted the sodden ball through them perhaps to the surprise of himself as much as of everybody else.

Final Score: All Blacks 9, North East Counties 3

Glasgow & Edinburgh

Hughenden, Glasgow, Tuesday, December 12, 1972
Attendance: 5,000

Teams and Scorers

All Blacks		Glasgow & Edinburgh		
Karam	C 2P	B. Hay	Boroughmuir FP	
Hales		R. S. M. Hannah	West of Scotland	
Robertson		M. D. Hunter	Glasgow HSFP	
Skudder		I. W. Forsyth	Stewart's Col FP	
		S. I. Briggs	Edinburgh Wanderers	
Sayers				
Burgess				
		F. N. F. Dall	Heriot's FP	T
Colling		D. W. Morgan (capt.)	Melville Col FP	2P
Matheson		J. Craig	Ayr	
Urlich	T	O. Dunlop	West of Scotland	
Lambert		D. S. D. McCallum	Jordanhill	
Macdonald		R. W. J. Wright	Edinburgh Wanderers	
Haden		R. S. Talbot	Watsonians	
Stewart		T. Young	West of Scotland	
Sutherland	T	G. M. Strachan	Jordanhill	
Wyllie (capt.)		W. S. Watson	Boroughmuir FP	
Sub:				
P. J. Whiting for Haden				
16 pts			**10 pts**	

Referee: A. Welsby (Lancashire)

The scoreline is misleading. It was in fact another very close
shave. Glasgow & Edinburgh having been ahead 4–3 at half-
time, they were for most of the second half (at 7–9 and 10–12)
within merely a penalty or a dropped goal of victory and it was
only in the sixth and final minute of injury time that the All
Blacks made the winning line look respectable.

It was a really poor show by the tourists. Granted it was
their already suspect mid-week side but the Cities are not the

sort of opposition to set the world on fire, especially when for this match six of their stars stood down pending Saturday's Scotland game.

With a feast of possession, from rucks and line-outs (24–10), the All Blacks' backs were ineffectual, partly through their own lack of initiative and partly through superb tackling. In the second half the All Blacks had no option but to play to the forwards to see if they could put possession to better advantage, but still the tourists couldn't dominate. It was the local backs who showed every indication of dominating, making penetrating attacks from make-shift situations.

Before the poorest crowd of the tour (what can be expected from soccer-mad Glasgow?), the All Blacks at once applied pressure and for the first quarter of an hour looked as though they had things well in hand. Then as the ball came out along their back line Robertson knocked on. Cities' centre Forsyth took the advantage, hacked ahead and his running mate Hunter got possession and made for the line. Tackled, he managed to squeeze the ball out to fly-half Dall, who forced his way over. A beautiful conversion attempt by Morgan from near touch just missed. (**All Blacks 0, Glasgow & Edinburgh 4**)

Ten minutes elapsed before the All Blacks retaliated. From an infringement in a ruck handy to the Glasgow & Edinburgh line, Karam put over the penalty. (**3–4**) He had a couple more unsuccessful attempts before the half was through, but it would have been an injustice if the All Blacks had gone ahead from these, since the Cities were doing all the bright things.

From a splendid catch by Morgan, Hannah set off on a crossfield run which had the New Zealand defence in confusion; Forsyth kicked ahead and Karam only just managed to stop Briggs getting to the ball for a try. Again Briggs just missed scoring when a pass to him from a quick pick-up by Strachan was knocked on with the line at his mercy. The All Blacks were lucky to be merely one point down at the break.

Half-time: All Blacks 3, Glasgow & Edinburgh 4

Five minutes from the re-start the All Blacks proved themselves capable of taking the lead but in a not very spectacular way. From a tap penalty near the Cities' line Colling was held when he tried to get over but from the ensuing ruck Ulrich got the ball and barged across. Karam converted. (**9–4**)

In the eleventh minute of this second spell from near halfway close to touch Morgan put over a massive penalty (**9–7**) and from then until the end of normal time we had the All Blacks clinging to that precious 2-point lead with the Cities constantly threatening to be the first Scottish side to beat a New Zealand team.

Winger Hay and then Dall made exciting breaks which almost provided the little crowd with an historic moment to tell everybody about for years to come. But after a minute of injury time the crowd went flat when a Karam penalty appeared to make things safe for the tourists. (**12–7**) In the fourth extra minute allowed another blockbuster of a penalty by Morgan had all the locals hopefully excited again (**12–10**) and we had that tenterhooks situation whereby the injury time ticks away and victory could still go either way.

In the sixth minute of injury time it looked as though it could be Glasgow & Edinburgh who would come out on top when at a line-out in an attacking position a long one was thrown out. Sayers, however, did a good bit of anticipating, got possession and ran 40 yards before being hauled down. A Scottish fly-hack to touch missed, Sutherland picked up and scrambled the try which provided the deceptive winning margin.

Final Score: All Blacks 16, Glasgow & Edinburgh 10

Scotland

Murrayfield, Saturday, December 15, 1972
Attendance: 50,000

Teams and Scorers

New Zealand		*Scotland*		
Karam	C	†A. R. Irvine	Heriot's FP	2P
Williams		W. C. C. Steele	Bedford	
Robertson		†R. W. Forsyth	Stewart's Col FP	
Batty	T	J. M. Renwick	Hawick	
		†D. Shedden	West of Scotland	
Parkinson				
†Stevens				
		†I. R. McGeechan	Headingley	D
Going	T	I. G. McCrae	Gordonians	
Whiting, G. J.		A. B. Carmichael	West of Scotland	
Norton		R. L. Clark	Edinburgh Wanderers	
Matheson		J. McLauchlan	Jordanhill	
Macdonald		G. L. Brown	West of Scotland	
Whiting, P. J.		A. F. McHarg	London Scottish	
Kirkpatrick (capt.)		M. A. MacEwan	Gala	
Scown		R. J. Arneil	Northampton	
Wyllie	T	P. C. Brown (capt.)	Gala	
Sub:				
†Lambert for Matheson				

14 pts   9 pts

Referee: G. Domercq (France)   †New cap

In this Test the All Blacks seemed determined to establish
themselves as The Team That Just Couldn't Dominate.
Besides their early defeats and close calls in secondary matches,
against Wales they had started by showing every evidence of
being the dominant side, only to be in grave danger of losing at
the end. Now at Murrayfield, after living in Scottish territory
for almost the whole of the first half and doing enough in the
second to show they were the better equipped team, they were
coming up to the final whistle in a situation whereby a penalty

or a snatched try by Scotland would have meant defeat. As it
turned out, it was they who snatched a try in injury time, again
giving their winning margin an air of respectability as on the
Tuesday against Glasgow & Edinburgh.

For Scotland it was a saga of muffed chances—backline
moves full of promise never realised because of mishandling, one
in particular stemming from the initiative of new full-back
Andy Irvine, who had the best debut of a full-back in international rugby since Keith Jarrett went mad in his first outing
for Wales. Irvine, 21-year-old Edinburgh University student,
fielded the All Black kick-off clean as a whistle and continued
throughout the match never to do anything wrong plus doing a
lot of things to gladden the hearts of those who love the classic
attacking full-back. One could feel sad for Arthur Brown (out
through injury) watching replacement Irvine indicate that if
he goes on like this he'll be one of Scotland's greatest full-back
finds.

McGeechan, another new cap, did sterling work in the
clearing kick department as well as contributing a beautifully
taken left-foot drop and the other two newcomers, Forsyth and
Shedden, also did well by the selectors. Individually, that is.
With the Scottish forwards (Arneil especially) fighting like
demons to get a share of possession for them, the back division
displayed an over-all lack of polish that wasted the scoring
opportunities that would have meant victory.

The All Black scrummaging had improved greatly, despite
the absence of the banished Murdoch and Matheson having to
go off early. The makeshift front row of Graham Whiting-
Norton-Lambert did wonders. The everywhere man Kirkpatrick played a captain's innings. Going, as ever trying to do
so much, found a lot of it coming off this time, including his
great Hancock-like try at the end. Wingers Williams and Batty,
always menacing, again demonstrated what a pity it was that
the ball could not be got to them more regularly. And it was
Faultless Karam again, once more indicating what a mature
performer he had developed into in the short time since the
tour opened.

The day was mild and windless and following one of the
worst renditions of the National Anthem ever performed in

public, the All Blacks kicked off deep into Scottish territory and remained parked there for most of the first spell. With both sides reluctant to use their backs the first-half pattern was very much scrum or line-out followed by a kick, Going and Stevens doing it in hopes of tactical advantage and the Scots' backs kicking to touch to relieve the pressure. Once Scotland did pass right along the backline, with Irvine joining in, and a good run momentarily took them out of their own half. Thirty minutes elapsed before the All Blacks risked the same sort of thing and Batty, almost visibly surprised at getting the ball in this way, set off infield and was stopped only with difficulty.

It looked as though the first half would just be written off as All Black pressure with nothing to show for it. But then in the fifth minute of injury time Williams, hellbent for the line, was brought to ground by a spectacular ankle dive by Shedden. Going got the ball from the ensuing scrum, went blind and passed to Wyllie. With the defenders converging on the corner flag, he saw a gap between them and the scrum. He speedily went through it. Karam converted.

Half-time: New Zealand 6, Scotland 0

Shortly after the restart Irvine began to imprint his name on the game. First he kicked a strong, high penalty from 35 yards near touch (6–3) and then with the All Blacks pressing again the ball was tossed to him in front of his posts. Knowing that ironically this is a good place from which to launch an attack he sidestepped three opponents and transferred to Renwick when he reached the 25. Renwick continued towards halfway and did the right thing in holding until he had not only attracted his opposite number but had also sucked in Batty from the wing. So there was Steele with the unoccupied touchline before him. But as the crowd rose to cheer on one of the fastest wings in the business who surely must have won this race to the line, Renwick delayed just that split second too long and his pass to Steele was knocked down. Poor Renwick. This blunder could keep him awake nights for years to come. It could have been 7–6 or even 9–6 to the Scots. Instead a Batty try shortly after this made it 10–3 to the tourists. It was a beautiful try, made by Robertson from nothing. In a general mess of players 20 yards out to the attackers' right of the Scots' posts, Robertson got possession, ran through a group of three tacklers, eluded a fourth and then ran left towards the posts. At length nailed, he let the ball drop to his feet and directed a superbly judged grubber kick to the line midway between touch and the posts. So well did Robertson execute this move that it was a certainty that Batty would beat Steele to the touchdown. (**10–3**)

Steele, as if to underline in red ink Renwick's bloomer, then proceeded to transfer play from the Scots' 25 to touch five yards from the New Zealand line by dint of a great solo run and kick ahead. From the line-out McGeechan put over his drop-kick. (**10-6**) Irvine put over a massive penalty from halfway (**10–9**) and thus with eleven minutes to go it was anybody's match.

The Scots tossed the ball about but promising back movements broke down through a misdirected final pass or just plain bad handling. It was just such sloppiness that was the Scots' ultimate downfall. Into injury time they could still win—if they kept the ball in play—and McHarg, being forced into touch on the halfway line, lobbed the ball somewhat wildly infield. Going snatched it from above his head and ran. With all Scotland up on attack, there was nobody to get back to stop his dive for the line after his 50-yard runaway.

Final Score: New Zealand 14, Scotland 9

Southern Counties

Iffley Road, Oxford, Wednesday, December 20, 1972
Attendance: 8,000

Terms and Scorers

All Blacks		*Southern Counties*		
Morris	2C P	S. Crabtree	Bristol	
Williams	2T	R. Ellis-Jones	London Welsh	
Hurst		R. O. P. Jones	Oxford	
Hales	T	I. Ray	Oxford	
		P. Cadle	Saracens	T
Sayers				
Stevens				
		D. Llewelyn	London Welsh	C
Colling		D. Spawforth	Army	
Whiting, G. J.		M. R. Hannell	Bristol	
Urlich		H. Mains	Richmond	
Clark		K. Richardson	Gloucester	
Haden	T	J. S. Jarrett	Gloucester	
Eliason		J. Harwood	Oxford	
Stewart		M. Marshall	Richmond	
Kirkpatrick (capt.)		S. Godfrey	Loughborough Colls	
Holmes		J. Vaughan (capt.)	London Welsh	
	23 pts			6 pts

Referee: C. G. P. Thomas (Wales)

When half-time came with the All Blacks 11–0 up, someone in the crowd shouted: 'You should have had 40!' This nutshelled the game. Against about the weakest opposition of the tour the All Blacks had so much possession that their backs should have been taking it in turn to score tries. Instead merely four in all were scored, the backs being worse than just lacking in enterprise. They were blatantly inefficient—standing flat-footed, kicking aimlessly, misdirecting passes and often as not passing so slowly as to invite interception. The local backs, under the influence of former Saracens and Hertfordshire coach Ken

Bartlett presented a much better picture, even if their main source of possession was from All Black mistakes and latching on to those slow-motion passes.

A local crowd doesn't particularly mind seeing their home side, of which not much is expected, being beaten by one of the big touring teams but they do expect their money's worth in the form of some sparkling, expert rugby by the tourists. This they didn't get and rightfully they went home feeling very much short-changed.

In a match unworthy of much comment the All Blacks took more than half an hour to score. Stevens for once did a tactical kick which made sense and Williams beat Cadle to the touch-down. **(All Blacks 4, Southern Counties 0)** Morris, who was to be the focal point of derision for some of his place-kicking efforts, managed a 40-yard penalty shortly afterwards. **(7–0)** Then just on half-time Colling broke from a tap penalty, his forwards won a ruck and Sayers put Hales over.

Half-time: All Blacks 11, Southern Counties 0

The rest of the scoring was confined to the third quarter. Williams followed up his own kick ahead to score. Morris converted. **(17–0)** Colling made an opening and sent Kirkpatrick upfield for Haden to go over. **(23–0)** Then for Southern Counties winger Cadle latched on to a poor pass by the All Black scrum-half, to touch down happily under the posts for Llewelyn to convert. **(23–6)**

In the last quarter a touring side can be expected to assert themselves against poor mid-week opposition. But not this time. It was Southern Counties who looked more likely to pile on more points, especially through the efforts of Ray. When he kicked over the N.Z. line he was only just beaten to the ball by Morris. Then he was unlucky not to hold a gift interception from Sayers with the line open in front of him.

Final Score: All Blacks 23, Southern Counties 6

Combined Services

Twickenham, Tuesday, December 26, 1972
Attendance: 12,000

Teams and Scorers

All Blacks		*Combined Services*		
Morris	2C 4P D	Tpr. A. S. Turk	Army	
Batty	T	Cpl. W. C. C. Steele	RAF	
Hurst		Capt. D. S. Boyle	Army	T
Scudder		2nd Lieut. P. M. Davies	Army	
		Sub-Lieut. G. P. Phillips	Navy	
Parkinson	T			
Burgess				
		P.O. G. Jones	Navy	
Colling		Cpl. D. Spawforth	Army	
Lambert		R.E.A. J. C. Ackerman	Navy	
Urlich		Inst. Lieut.		
		R. L. Clarke	Navy	
Clark		Flt. Lieut.		
		J. Young (capt.)	RAF	
Whiting, P. J.		Fg. Off. P. J. Larter	RAF	2P
Eliason		Sgt. I. Cairns	Army	
Holmes		Lieut. A. J. W.		
		Higginson	Marines	
Scown	T	Lieut. L. C. P. Merrick	Navy	
Wyllie (capt.)		Lieut. P. J. Bird	Army	
		Sub:		
		Cpl. D. R. Fulford (Marines) for Ackerman		

31 pts   10 pts

Referee: N. P. Jones (Gloucester)

There's a story about W. G. Grace being skittled out first ball by a young bowler new to first-class cricket. 'Not out!' shouted the umpire. The bowler looked at him aghast. Explained the umpire: 'This crowd came to watch Grace bat, not to see you bowl him out.'

There was some sort of parallel in this match. It was a

holiday game. The crowd had come to see the All Blacks throw
the ball about, not to watch Trevor Morris taking endless shots
at goal to try to regain his place-kicking confidence. By the end
there were boos, catcalls, slow-handclapping as yet again
captain-for-the-day Wyllie would decide against a tap penalty
in favour of another Morris goal attempt.

Had it been a major fixture, Morris would have emerged a
hero, with his 19 excellent points from four penalties, two
conversions and a beautifully struck drop. Also he regained his
all-round confidence (lost through lack of match play after
injury) and showed the crowd, had they been interested, what a
class full-back he is. His high, bold touch kicks were superb,
two in particular each over 70 yards.

The Services did their best, got some good clean line-out
possession mainly through Larter, and their backs showed much
more enterprise than the tourists'—which was getting to be a
commonplace on this tour.

From the outset Burgess let it be known that he was going
to kick. On a windless, dry, perfect day for handling, God alone
knows why. And his tactical kicking was to such little effect
that 35 minutes had elapsed before they opened their score.
Even then it wasn't through the backs making the most of all
the good ball they were getting. Morris put over a penalty
from an easy position (**All Blacks 3, Combined Services 0**),
thus blighting Services' hopes of reaching the turn-around 0–0.
Worse was to come. Morris goaled again from the 10-yard line
(**6–0**) and then from near touch 35 yards out put over his high
and true drop. (**9–0**) But it was in injury time that real disaster
came for the Services. Unwisely indulging in passing on their
own line, Spawforth at length decided the time had come to
clear—and miscued right into the arms of Batty a mere dozen
yards out. This gift try (**13–0**) made the score line flattering to
the All Blacks, whose first-half display was not worth that.

Half-time: All Blacks 13, Combined Services 0

On resumption the tourists had obviously had a pep talk,
for at once Burgess ran the ball and put Batty over under the
posts—unfortunately disallowed because his pass was forward.
But two minutes later Hurst, clearly grateful at getting the ball

along the line, weaved his way through a batch of defenders and gave Parkinson a try at the posts. Morris converted. (**19–0**) Now it would be thought that the floodgates were open. But the Services kept up their fight, rewarded by a massive Larter penalty from 52 yards. (**19–3**) Morris responded (**22–3**) and again Larter goaled a 50-yarder. (**22–6**)

However, the slim hopes were dashed when Morris, to the tune of slow handclaps notched his fourth penalty. (**25–6**) With that unassailable lead, surely now we'd see some sparkling stuff from the visitors. But no, it was Services who had the crowd on its feet. Inside his own half centre Davies knocked down a Scudder kick and with a succession of kicks ahead and fumbling attempts to pick up the ball eventually fell on it 60 yards later behind the N.Z. line. The referee, communing with nature on the halfway line at the time, ran like the wind to the point of action to signal the try. There could have been at least one Davies knock-on and there was some doubt as to whether he grounded properly, but even though the onlookers were a bit self-conscious about it, it was double figures for the Services. (**25–10**)

Not until just on time did the All Blacks turn on the sort of stuff expected regularly from New Zealand touring teams. A forwards-and-backs assault was launched by Holmes, who transferred to Burgess, who in turn linked with Scown, for the flanker to take a couple of tacklers over the line with him under the posts. Morris converted (**31–10**), leaving everyone unhappy there hadn't been more of that type of thing throughout the match.

Final Score: All Blacks 31, Combined Services 10

East Glamorgan

Cardiff Arms Park, Saturday, December 30, 1972
Attendance: 25,000

Teams and Scorers

All Blacks		East Glamorgan		
Karam	C 2P	C. Bolderson	Pontypridd	P
Williams		D. Schick	Brigend	
Robertson		I Hopkins	Cardiff Coll of Ed	P
Hales	2T	I. Hall	South Wales Police	
		V. Jenkins	Brigend	
Hurst				
Stevens	T			
		R. Evans	South Wales Police	D
Going		G. Evans	South Wales Police	
Whiting, G. J.		J. Lloyd (capt.)	Brigend	
Norton		C. Lewis	Glam Wanderers	
Lambert		A. Davies	South Wales Police	
Macdonald		B. Howe	Maestag	
Whiting, P. J.		P. Williams	Brigend	
Holmes		G. Jones	Bridgend	
Kirkpatrick (capt.)		D. Brain	Brigend	
Sutherland		R. Dudley-Jones	Cardiff Coll of Ed	
Sub:		*Sub:*		
Clark for Whiting, G. J.		D. John (Pontypridd) for G. Evans		
	20 pts			9 pts

Referee: K. Clark (Ireland)

It was the *Daily Telegraph*'s John Reason who said that 'the spectators should have been charged half price because they could see only half the match.' This was literally true. The blanket of fog that hung over the Arms Park never lifted as much as the authorities had hoped it would and at best all that those in the two big stands on either side could see was to midfield.

From the pressbox side highlights were glimpsed such as the first Hales try, a splendid run by Kirkpatrick of the type which now has his brand name on it and the Sid Going punch-up. But as to an overall picture of the match, this of necessity had to be a reconstruction from talking to people afterwards.

The Going affair, which is dealt with more fully elsewhere in this book, consisted to Going blatantly obstructing Ron Evans following up a kick, East Glamorgan players converging on Going and scuffling with him and finally Going punching Gareth Evans to such effect that he had to be taken to hospital for twelve facial stitches. Spectators in a position to see the fracas shouted 'Off! Off! Off!' Referee Clark instead gave Going a talking to which lasted several minutes.

The match was a pretty meaningless one from the start. (To the outside world, who or what is East Glamorgan? Far Better for the All Blacks to have been playing Swansea.) It was made additionally meaningless by the fog. However, the hodge-podge local selection played well enough to be in a 9–10 position after half-time before the All Blacks groped through to an undistinguished victory—'I had hoped for a better all-round performance' said skipper Kirkpatrick.

The home side went into the lead after four minutes from a 25-yard Bolderson penalty. (**All Blacks 0, East Glamorgan 3**) But nine minutes later Karam wiped this out with a 20-yarder. (**3–3**) Then came the first Hales try, which stemmed from a left-wing blind side break by Going, who attracted several defenders before transferring to Hales, who got past three tacklers in all to score a good winger's try. (**7–3**) An easy Karam penalty in front of the posts (**10–3**) was followed by the unusual event of the locals rather than the All Blacks winning the ball from a ruck, for Ron Evans to put over a beautiful drop from 35 yards out near touch.

Half-time: All Blacks 10, East Glamorgan 6

Ray Williams, Welsh coaching organiser, on the other side of the field from the pressbox, did his best to keep everyone informed over the loud speakers and he was to announce shortly after the re-start that Hopkins had kicked a penalty. (**10–9**) It turned out that it had been for a Clark late tackle on Bolderson. All that was seen by the press of how the All Blacks' next six points were scored was the conversion going through

ANYONE FOR BALLET? Ripley and Sutherland do a *pas de deux* in a line-out during the England International at Twickenham.

BOB BURGESS showed himself as a brilliant running fly-half when he chose to – or was allowed to – as in the opening game against Western Counties (*below, left*) but to the disappointment of those who knew what an exciting player he could be, there was far too much of this (*below, right*).

A PERFECT HANDSPRING by Mike Parkinson against Western Counties, who unfortunately did not live up later to his great showing in this match. This sequence of shots furnished a good example of the improvement of rugby photography in Britain, thanks to a new breed of photographers who have

PETER WHITING, who was to earn himself the reputation of the best all-round forward in the side – in the tight as a lock, at the line-out and in the loose.

broken with the conventional portraying of nothing much more than line-outs, tries and conversions. Chris Smith took these and some of the others of the best shots in this book.

ANDY HADEN, with dropped shoulder and ball at his side, gives English 'collapsed ruck' forwards an object lesson in how to enter such a situation.

A memorable – and rare – piece of clever All Black midfield play among the backs when Robertson (with ball) and Burgess inter-passed to bring one of the eight tries against Midland Counties East.

In the fog-shrouded farce that was the East Glamorgan match, spectators saw literally only half the match – from where they were watching to the centre of the field. Onlookers on the other side of Cardiff Arms Park saw nothing of this Stevens try.

the posts. Apparently Stevens had gone over near the corner flag from a Going break, with Karam adding the extras. (**16–9**)

The last try apparently came when the tourists, having unsuccessfully essayed a dummy No. 8 move, tried it again and succeeded when Going put Hales over in the same corner.

Final Score: All Blacks 20, East Glamorgan 9

South Western Counties

Redruth, Tuesday, January 2, 1972
Attendance: 20,000

Teams and Scorers

All Blacks		South Western Counties		
Morris		R. S. Staddon	Exeter	
Batty	3T	K. C. Plummer	Bristol	T
Hurst	2T	T. Palmer (capt.)	Gloucester	
Hales		B. Friend	Plymouth Albion	
		R. Warmington	St Luke's Coll	
Sayer				
Burgess	T			
		N. Bennett	St Luke's Coll	
Colling		A. F. Pearn	Bristol	P
Lambert	C	D. Hosking	Hayle	
Urlich		J. Lockyer	Exeter	
Clark		P. Baxter	Exeter	
Eliason		J. Scott	Exeter	
Haden		J. Baxter	Exeter	
Kirkpatrick (capt.)	T	A. Cole	Exeter	
Stewart		P. J. Hendy	St Ives	
Wyllie		A. Hollins	Bedford	
30 pts				7 pts

Referee: E. M. Lewis (Wales)

This was more like it. More like the running in of tries in the
All Blacks' opening match of the tour. The 19th match was a
bit late to remind us of those high hopes they had raised of
their being an entertaining side to watch. In fact in this game
they even left it a bit later to turn on the really spectacular
stuff, four of their seven tries being piled on in the last eight
minutes.

The South West had fought stoutly through the first period
and early in the second they had their moments of ascendancy.
Only 4–3 down at half-time, they could well have been ahead

if Alan Pearn, normally a notable points scorer with the boot, had not chosen this as one of his off days. Had he kicked merely half of his nine attempts, instead of just slotting one, it would have been a morale booster for his side and if it had not actually brought them victory at least it would have prevented them from disintegration at the end.

Morris was equally off target, failing with all seven of his shots at goal. One felt sorry for him. With this match all thoughts of his reinstating himself as full-back in any of the remaining Tests were gone.

Star of the match was undoubtedly Grant Batty—not only for his hat-trick of tries but also for his terrier-like determination to get possession away from his opponents and for his copybook low tackling.

The All Blacks were parked on the South West doorstep from the kick-off and were kept out partially through solid tackling but mainly through lack of imagination as to how to get the key to the door. When they did score there was an element of luck to it. A long Morris kick to the corner flag failed to get there but full-back Staddon unfortunately fumbled it into touch. With their throw-in to a line-out on the home team's line an All Black try was on and it was duly provided by Morris coming into the threequarters and chipping ahead for Batty to win the race over the line. (**All Blacks 4, South West Counties 0**)

For the rest of the half there was nothing much between the two sides and this was confirmed by a 30-yard Pearn penalty to bring the margin to one point.

Half-time: All Blacks 4, South West Counties 3

There was also a measure of luck in the All Blacks' next try, shortly after the restart, when some confused handling on the South West line allowed Burgess to snap up the ball and go over. (**8–3**) But it was now very much even-steven and a chance was missed to have the All Blacks in trouble when Pearn flunked three penalties in as many minutes. This clearly disheartened the South-Westerners and they let Hurst through to draw Staddon and time his pass perfectly to Batty, who went in unopposed. Surprisingly the conversion attempt was given to prop

Lambert and equally surprisingly he hoisted it beautifully
between the posts from near touch. (**14-3**)

This was the cue for another of the rare occasions on which
these All Blacks let themselves go. First Hurst scored when
Plummer fumbled a Burgess diagonal kick. (**18-3**) Then with
Plummer submerged in a ruck Colling was smart enough to
work the vacant blind side and the ball eventually came infield
for Kirkpatrick to sail over. (**22-3**) Batty got his third when
Morris joined the line after a midfield dummy scissors. (**26-3**)
And then came the All Blacks' seventh and final try, one of
the best they scored on the tour.

From loose play after a line-out Lambert picked up and
handed to Colling. He spun a long one to Batty, who had come
infield to first five-eighth, and he sent across an equally long
pass to Burgess. who flicked it to Kirkpatrick (withdrawn from
the line-out). Kirkpatrick did a lovely dummy and then when
challenged missed out Hurst and threw it over his head to
Morris. The full-back could have gone through on his own but
unselfishly made sure of things by passing infield to Hurst for
for his second try. (**30-3**)

Watching this gem, one could not help but feel: they could
do it when they wanted to, why didn't they want to more often?

Now playing with abandon, it wasn't surprising that the All
Blacks up on attack left a gap for Plummer to end the proceedings with a consolation try for the home side.

Final Score: All Blacks 30, South West Counties 7

England

Twickenham, Saturday, January 6, 1973
Attendance: 72,000

Teams and Scorers

New Zealand		England	
Karam	C	S. A. Doble	Moseley
Williams	D	A. J. Morley	Bristol
Robertson		P. S. Preece	Coventry
Batty		†P. J. Warfield	Durham U
		D. J. Duckham	Coventry
Parkinson			
Stevens			
		J. F. Finlan	Moseley
Going		J. G. Webster	Moseley
Whiting, G. J.		G. B. Stevens	Penzance
Norton		J. V. Pullin (capt.)	Bristol
Lambert		†W. F. Anderson	Orrell
Macdonald		P. J. Larter	Northampton
Whiting, P. J.		C. W. Ralston	Richmond
Wyllie		J. A. Watkins	Gloucester
Kirkpatrick (capt.)	T	A. Neary	Broughton Park
Sutherland		A. G. Ripley	Rosslyn Park
9 pts			0 pts

Referee: J. Young (Scotland)　　†New cap

For England if was a match of 'if onlys'. If only Preece had held Duckham's pass for a certain try at the close of the first half. If only Preece's second-half try had not been disallowed. If only Sam Doble had landed even *one* of his four kickable penalties.

England played with zest, fire and imagination. Their supporters could argue that if only they had got some sort of score on the board in the course of the match it would have given them that extra lift that could have meant eventual victory. The over-all picture of the game was of English backs and forwards playing like demons, running all over the paddock in their effort to score, while New Zealand remained relatively static, merely frustrating their aims. With their early 6-point lead from a Kirkpatrick try they had the psychological advantage of the opponents having to score twice to win. New Zealand's supporters could argue that if England *had* come within closer range on the scoreboard, the All Blacks had the necessary in hand to triumph over them.

In the line-outs England had parity (equally sharing the 46 decisive ones) : in the loose Stevens, Ralston, Neary and Ripley were often to be seen powering their way upfield individually. But when it came to capitalising on this fair share of the run of the play, the perhaps over-eager England backs always contrived to botch things up at the last moment, partially through their own mistakes, to a great extent through solid N.Z. tackling. In this connection magnificent little Batty was at it again. One in particular—when he came infield to nail Warfield so effectively that the 3-stone heavier England centre, going full out forward, found himself propelled backwards at the impact of the Mighty Atom.

On slippery turf from morning drizzle, England indicated from the outset that they meant business. Duckham, lying deep, came through like the Coventry Inter-City and could well have continued to the All Black line if he hadn't been obstructed when taking his pass. Then the English Stevens from a line-out sent Ripley away up midfield, to have the jampacked crowd for once giving their team the sort of vocal support more common to Cardiff Arms Park than Twickers.

But then Going, whose role as the All Blacks linchpin was to be glowingly crowned with success in this match, kicked two very good touch-finders which took New Zealand to within striking distance. He fielded a long one over the end of a line-out and was given extra room to work by Neary inadvertently going to ground as he went to block him. Going transferred to Wyllie in front of the posts. He was held but the ball popped out of the ruck, for Kirkpatrick to pick it up and dab it over the line next to the posts for the easiest of tries. Karam converted. **(New Zealand 6, England o)**

The score after eight minutes dictated the pattern for the

rest of the match and one was reminded somewhat of the Springboks' early 5–0 lead at the same ground in 1961, when no amount of throwing the ball about by England could overcome the deficit. Again England were doing the same thing, with the same failure to finish. Doble could have changed the whole terms of reference with penalties in the 18th, 27th and 30th minutes. As to his all-round full-back play, it was good enough at this stage. He twice made a good sally from a defensive position, for example, and he was able to block Batty when he made an electrifying 50-yard run along the touchline. But in the very department which, after all, was the prime reason he was in the side he sadly let England down.

Finlan almost pulled off the elusive England try which at all times seemed on the cards. From loose play near touch in the N.Z. 25 he dummied a giant pass inland and then set off on a crafty little dash to the corner flag. But unluckily he just hadn't managed entirely to hoodwink the defence.

Webster seemed to be there where he followed a kick over the New Zealand line but in the scramble for the ball Williams managed to kick it dead.

Then from the five-yard scrum Finlan lay back deep, clearly in the drop-kick position. But instead he sent it along the threes and Duckham had the crowd screaming as he made for the line. He tried to sidestep his way infield through the defence. He was baulked, but Preece running around behind him had a try for the taking along the vacant touchline. The disastrous dropped pass was the result of Duckham, off balance, sending the slippery ball out awkwardly.

Half-time: New Zealand 6, England 0

As the second spell started there was a newsworthy event— from a scrum the ball went by hand right out along the New Zealand backline to the wing. But the novelty of receiving the ball in this fashion was too much for Bryan Williams. He dropped it. This was the first time in the match that the All Blacks had attempted this manoeuvre and they seemed wary to try it again. Following the half-time chat Going was now sending out to the backs from time to time rather than his almost exclusively 9-man rugby of the first half. But the ball seldom got past the five-eighths before there was the so familiar All Black high punt.

For their part, England continued to move the ball at every opportunity and from one such passing session Preece, encountering a cluttered field over on his right, doubled back to the other side, where he linked with Ripley. Play was taken to the New Zealand posts. England won the ruck and it was a scoring set-up as Warfield tossed out a high pass to Preece to avoid the clutching defenders. Preece tapped it down and caught it and dived over. I can't remember such an ear-piercing crowd reaction at Twickenham—only for it to switch to groans as the try was disallowed. Few could figure out why, since under the new Laws the ball hadn't be knocked on by Preece. As it turned out, Warfield's pass had been fractionally forward and there could be no argument with Referee Jake Young's decision afterwards, when the TV replay confirmed it. Young had been dead right—as with another disallowed try, by New Zealand later. There was no doubt about the accuracy of his refereeing. Only complaint one might level at him was an over alacrity to whistle up each error, rarely letting play go on for the possible advantage.

It went without saying that an England try at that stage—fifteen minutes into the second half—could have made all the difference. As it was, four minutes later they suffered a disaster when a Finlan clearance was miscued into the arms of Williams who, with all the time in the world, put over a beautiful drop (9-0) and that, as the Americans say, was your ball game.

England kept trying manfully. They survived a typical Kirkpatrick run which took him over for a try, confirmed by TV afterwards as correctly disallowed through his grounding the ball before getting over the line.

In the dying minutes Doble incurred the displeasure of the crowd by kicking for touch when keeping the ball in play was essential. But in those last twenty minutes it just didn't seem 'on' for England to penetrate the rigid New Zealand defence and do the amount of scoring necessary for victory. It became something of an anti-climax. It was three-quarters of a great match.

Final Score: New Zealand 9, England 0

MATCH NO. 21

Newport

Rodney Parade, Newport, Wednesday, January 10, 1973
Attendance: 20,000

Teams and Scorers

All Blacks		Newport	
Morris	2P	R. Williams	C 2P D
Williams	2P T	G. Fuller	
Robertson		G. Talbot	
Skudder		N. Edwards	
		P. Ward	
Sayers	T		
Burgess			
		D. Rogers	
Going (capt.)		A. Evans	
Whiting, G. J.		I. Barnard	
Urlich		G. Williams	
McNicol		B. Rowland	
Whiting, P. J.		L. Jones	
Eliason		J. Watkins	T
Scown		P. Watts	
Holmes		G. Evans (capt.)	
Wyllie		J. Jeffrey	
	20 pts		15 pts

Referee: Air-Commodore G. C. Lamb

It was a very exciting match, the All Blacks yet again allowing themselves to be in the position whereby the home side could have snatched victory in the dying minutes.

Also it was an unruly match. Referee Lamb could well have sent off four players—three All Blacks (Wyllie, Going and Peter Whiting) and Newport lock Lyn Jones. Wyllie, ever a chatty soul, was warned by 'Larry' Lamb for telling him how to do his job. Going, having been warned for persistent croked put-in, had a comment to make about it and was let off with ten yards added to a penalty. Whiting and Jones turned on one of the oddest sights ever to be seen in major rugby. With the play on one side of the field there they were all alone on the other side, locked in conflict like two characters in a Western fighting it out on the ground after they'd run out of bullets. This combined with the two front rows shaping up to each other on more than one occasion made it a brawling affair in which the standard of rugby was as low as the tension was high.

Newport, having already lost 13 matches this season and being without four of their stars, surprised everybody by making it such a closely contested match. Urged on by their fanatical supporters they stormed to the All Blacks line from the kick-off and in the first three minutes were unlucky not to do a repeat of the early Llanelli try. They did in fact score first, with a Robin Williams 38 yard penalty in the seventh minute. **(All Blacks 0, Newport 3)** Their lead was short-lived, however. Morris equalised from about the same distance three minutes later. **(3–3)**

The fact that the penalties came thick and fast was an obvious reflection of what was happening on field—more rough-and-tumble then rugby. In the 13th minute Morris put over another **(6–3)** and then Robin Williams just failed with two huge attempts from halfway. Being an ambipedester (if there's no such word, you know what I mean), the Newport full-back switched to his left foot for the next one, from shorter range, and was successful.

Half-time: All Blacks 6, Newport 6

Morris having gone astray with a couple more penalties before half-time, the All Blacks' next shot at goal three minutes into the second spell was given to Bryan Williams, who was there with one from 10 yards outside the Newport 25 in front of the posts. **(9–6)**

It was just after this that Whiting and Jones had their eyeball-to-eyeball confrontation and this venting of feelings had the effect of quietening things down somewhat, so that we now started to see some constructive rugby. From in front of the Newport posts Burgess tossed a long one out to Skudder, who looked as though he would be forced into touch, but as the defence converged on him he flicked a very well judged pass infield for Sayers to score. **(13–6)**

Over on the other wing Bryan Williams appeared to be set for a try, only to be brought down by a great tackle by Watkins. The winger, however, put the All Blacks further ahead with the game's sixth penalty. (**16–6**)

Constantly exciting, it was now Newport's turn to go on the attack and when a forward rush nearly took them over, Wyllie sent out a poor clearance. Robin Williams fielded it on the 25 and dropped a goal. (**16–9**

With five minutes to go it looked as though the All Blacks would be able to get home all right and they appeared to make things absolutely safe when they were presented with a lucky try. With Newport pressing, scrum-half Evans had to go back to retrieve a bad ball and threw a wild pass infield. Robertson intercepted and sent Burgess away up the middle. When challenged near the Newport 25 he lobbed a long one out to Bryan Williams, who scampered over. (**20–9**)

Now into injury time, we got a wonderful example of how much more interesting the game had been made by the increase in value of a try from 3 to 4 points. In the old days the tourists' 11-point lead would have made them pretty well unassailable at this stage. But Edwards made a break to the All Blacks' line and Watkins scored from the ruck, for Robin Williams to convert. (**20–15**) Now, thanks to the new scoring values, Newport were in a position to win. All they needed to do was snatch another try and convert it. But despite all the yelled encouragement from their supporters, they just couldn't manage it.

Final Score: All Blacks 20, Newport 15

Midland Counties (East)

Welford Road, Leicester, Saturday, January 13, 1972
Attendance: 20,000

Teams and Scorers

All Blacks		Midland Counties (East)		
Karam	4C P	D. F. Whibley	Leicester	C 2P
Hales		M. J. Duggan	Leicester	
Robertson	T	M. Yandle	Leicester	
Batty	T	G. Phillips	Northampton	
		R. Morris	Northampton	
Hurst	T			
Burgess	T			
		B. Jones	Leicester	
Colling	T	J. A. Allen	Leicester	T
Whiting, G. J.		D. L. Powell (capt.)	Northampton	
Norton		P. J. Wheeler	Leicester	
Clark		P. Duffy	Northampton	
Haden		P. J. Larter	Northampton	
Macdonald		R. M. Wilkinson	Cambridge U	
Stewart	T	C. J. Baynes	Leicester	
Sutherland	T	G. J. Adey	Leicester	
Kirkpatrick (capt.)	T	I. Clayton	Notts	
		Sub:		
		A. B. C. Davies (Notts) for Jones		

43 pts   12 pts

It had certainly been a long wait from the first match of the tour to the 22nd for the All Blacks fully to live up to the promise of that opening game. This day they turned on a scintillating display of open rugby, running in eight crowd-pleasing tries and notching their highest score yet.

The home pack had something like equality in the set scrums but in every other phase of forward play they were outclassed, which meant a feast of possession for Colling, with that great spin pass of his, to send the backs away time and time again.

As one headline summed it up very neatly: NO GOING . . .
SO IT'S ALL GO.

Stewart got things under way with a try at the posts when
the defence were in confusion dealing with a Burgess kick ahead.
Karam converted. (**All Blacks 6, Midland Counties East 0**)
Burgess then further confused the home side by switching from
the tactical kicking they expected of him to running through
one his own, for Karam again to convert. (**12–0**)

The Counties had their moment of glory when centre Yandle
changed direction over to the right wing, where Duggan had a
great run, with support on hand when he was blocked. Allen
took the inside pass to score, Whibley converting. (**12–6**) But
the fillip to the local morale didn't last long. A blindside sally
by Burgess found Kirkpatrick ready to go over, and Karam
having converted, the All Blacks came to the break with a
healthy lead.

Half-time: All Blacks 18, Midland Counties East 6

A Karam penalty which brought his points total for the tour
past the century mark was the only score in the third quarter
(**21–6**), and then Robertson opened the floodgates with a
brilliant try following a clever exchange with Burgess of the
type of ingenious midfield backplay for which the tourists had
not been noted. (**25–6**) A Whibley penalty merely interrupted
for a moment the flow of tries (**25–9**), the next one coming from
Colling, converted by Karam, when the said Whibley dropped
a pass on his own line. (**31–9**) Another show of local defiance
in the form of a further Whibley penalty (**31–12**) was followed
by Burgess making an opening for Sutherland. (**35–12**)

Then we saw two of the outstanding tries of the tour. First
Robertson was brilliantly elusive, interpassing with Hurst as
they progressed down the right-hand side, for the latter at
length to dive over. (**39–12**) Then Batty rounded things off
dramatically when Hurst thrust through and sent him off
along the left touchline. As one onlooker commented, he was
like a fizzing firecracker as he covered more than 40 yards
to score, with no defender having an earthly chance of laying
a hand on him.

Final Score: All Blacks 43, Midland Counties East 12

Munster

Musgrave Park, Cork, Tuesday, January 16, 1973
Attendance: 12,000

Teams and Scorers

All Blacks		*Munster*		
Morris	P	T. J. Kiernan (capt.)	Cork Constitution	
Williams		P. Parfrey	UCC	
Hales		F. P. K. Bresnihan	London Irish	
Skudder		S. Dennison	Garryowen	
		J. Barry	Dolphin	
Parkinson				
Stevens				
		B. J. McGann	Cork Constitution	P
Colling		D. Canniffe	Cork Constitution	
McNicol		P. O'Callaghan	Dolphin	
Urlich		J. Leahy	Cork Constitution	
Lambert		K. Keyes	Sunday's Well	
Haden		M. Keane	UCC	
Eliason		J. Madigan	Bohemians	
Wyllie (capt.)		J. Buckley	Sunday's Well	
Sutherland		T. Moore	Highfield	
Holmes		S. Deering	Garryowen	
	3 pts			3 pts

Referee: D. W. Jones (England)

As the Irish said, Munster won this match everywhere but on the scoreboard. And one had to agree with them. Coached by Noel Murphy, who had been preparing for this game since the opening of the season, Munster contained the All Black forwards, had the defence at sixes-and-sevens through judicious kicks, mostly by fly-half McGann, and with ramrod tackling by centres Bresnihan and Dennison gave the tourists' backs few opportunities to get within striking distance of the Munster line. Scrum-half Donal Canniffe could be regarded as the man of the match by virtue of his faultless link between the forwards, of whom Terry Moore was the most prominent, and the tactical McGann.

Granted it was very much the All Blacks' B team but even such Test players as Wyllie and Sutherland weren't allowed the scope really to assert themselves and Stevens had such an atrocious day of mishandling and miskicking that he succeeded in nothing but dumping himself out of the Test side for Saturday's Ireland match.

The standard of rugby for the record crowd at Musgrave Park was not high but the mounting excitement as Munster played their hearts out to hold on to McGann's penalty lead made up for that. With visions of the first win against the All Blacks by an Irish side it was a cruel disappointment for them when they were robbed of victory by the Trevor Morris equaliser in injury time.

The tourists could have made things relatively safe for themselves early in the first half with three kickable penalties but Morris and Williams shared the misses and captain for the day Wyllie despaired of getting points on the board that way, running the ball when the fourth easy penalty presented itself. For his part, McGann, also missed one in the first half, which was a rugged affair, with several warnings from Referee Jones. He tended to come down more heavily on Munster than on the visitors, as indicated by the awarding of 20–9 penalties against them throughout the game.

Half-time: All Blacks o, Munster o

Barry McGann set things alight in the 9th minute of the second spell with a 40-yard penalty (**0–3**) and in an effort to fight back the All Blacks had one of their few cohesive back movements, which could have snatched the lead for them if Skudder had not knocked on when the overlap gave him nothing to do but touch down.

The All Blacks were at panic stations as the second half wore on and whatever they did they seemed quite unable to break the stranglehold Noel Murphy's demons had on the game. And then, with the match a minute into injury time, Wyllie made a decision for which he will be forever thankful.

At a ruck 30 yards out from the Munster line prop Phil

O'Callaghan was caught stopping the ball from coming out on the All Black side and Wyllie had to decide whether to run it or give Trevor Morris one more change to live up to his goal-kicking reputation. He chose the latter and luckily for the All Blacks poor Morris at last managed to salvage something from his unhappy tour.

Final Score: All Blacks 3, Munster 3

Ireland

Lansdowne Road, Dublin, Saturday, January 20, 1973
Attendance: 50,000

Teams and Scorers

New Zealand		*Ireland*		
Karam	C	T. J. Kiernan (capt.)	Cork Constitution	
Williams		T. O. Grace	St Mary's Coll	T
Robertson		M. K. Flynn	Wanderers	
Batty		C. M. H. Gibson	NIFC	
		A. W. McMaster	Ballymena	
†Hurst				
Burgess		B. J. McGann	Cork Constitution	2P
Going	T	J. J. Moloney	St Mary's Coll	
Lambert		J. F. Lynch	St Mary's Coll	
Norton		J. W. Kennedy	London Irish	
Whiting, G. J.		R. J. McLoughlin	Blackrock Coll	
Macdonald		†K. M. A. Mays	Univ Coll Dublin	
Whiting, P. J.		W. J. McBride	Ballymena	
Wyllie	T	J. F. Slattery	Blackrock Coll	
Sutherland		T. A. P. Moore	Highfield	
Kirkpatrick (capt.)		J. C. Davidson	Dungannon	
	10 pts			10 pts

Referee: M. Joseph (Wales)   †New cap

This Test divided itself into three sections. In the first phase Ireland, with a howling wind behind them, were on the attack with both forwards and backs working well and their 3–0 lead from a penalty was well deserved. In the middle section, the longest of the three, the All Blacks were clearly the dominant force and looked safe to coast to victory on the 10–3 lead they had built up. Then in the final phase of ten thrilling minutes, Ireland fought back to snatch the draw.

There was a parallel with the England match, when New Zealand rode along on a handy lead without pressing home their dominance by increasing it. Kirkpatrick after this Irish Test said his team hadn't been coasting. But the fact remains that they seemed to be content, with kicks down the wind, to keep Ireland penned in their own territory. No attempt was made to send the ball out to their wings for tries which one felt were there for the taking. Williams saw virtually nothing of the ball. The couple of good runs Batty had were very much of his own making.

But where this game differed from the England one was in Ireland, against the odds, producing some Celtic fire for a grandstand finish of the type England just wasn't capable of.

The record sell-out crowd for an Ireland match against a touring side did much to spur on that great finish and when their team all but pulled off a win there were scenes of excitement on the field rarely equalled before at Lansdowne Road.

From the All Blacks' kick-off Ireland at once rushed things into New Zealand territory and, as had been expected, their pack at this stage completely outscrummaged their opponents. After eight minutes New Zealand were penalised at the scrum and from 48 yards Barry McGann goaled. (**New Zealand o, Ireland 3**)

But as the game got into the second quarter the All Blacks had settled down and their good rucking and improved scrummaging forced Ireland back. In the 29th minute Ireland heeled from a scrum 20 yards out from their line, Moloney's possession was spoiled and Going got hold of the ball from the ruck to score a try which has now come to be regarded as 'typical Going'. There were five defenders within range to stop his progress to the line but by sheer strength and determination he dodged and shook them off. Karam converted.

Half-time: New Zealand 6, Ireland 3

With the advantage of the wind, it was all New Zealand pressure as the second spell got under way and after 18 minutes there was a beautifully executed try completed by Wyllie. On their own 25 Flynn and Grace were in a mix-up as to who would retrieve the ball and Sutherland solved things for them by grabbing it himself. He sent Burgess away on the short side and it was beautiful to watch the way the New Zealand first five-eighth, knowing he couldn't make the corner flag, poised himself for the inside pass to Wyllie, coming through at full throttle. Kiernan, on hand to impede Wyllie, was completely bowled over. (**10–3**)

A 7-point deficit with both the All Black machine and the wind to contend with seemed too much, but then with a bare ten minutes to go, Kiernan changed the whole terms of reference. In trouble on his 25 he elected to open up instead of kicking for touch and a weaving run took him 30 yards upfield. Gibson carried on the move and when challenged by Wyllie he kicked ahead. Sutherland fielded and seemed relieved to be able to get the ball into touch. Ireland's throw-in was crooked, but so was Going's put-in at the ensuing scrum and McGann's successful penalty got a tumultuous reception. (**10–6**)

With but five minutes to go, Ireland put everything they had into it. The All Blacks' safe lead was no longer safe and yet again they were going into the final stages of a match with defeat a possibility.

The All Black kick-off after McGann's penalty went straight into touch. Ireland won the heel and from the ruck which followed a kick ahead Moloney got possession and sent Grace away on the right wing. New Zealand's disrupted defence left him with only Karam to beat. Rather than risking a tackle he kicked over his head and Irish hearts dropped when it looked very much as though the ball was going to go over the deadball line. Grace, however, kept streaking after it and won the touchdown race with what appeared to be just a matter of inches to spare.

The crowd erupted, many of them on to the field. A try that would be talked about in Ireland for years. All that was needed now was for McGann to complete the *coup de grace* with a conversion. Rarely has there been such a silence at a rugby ground as he ran up to kick. The cheering started as it was seen to be going straight and true between the posts, only for the jubilation to be cut short as the wind just swung it outside the left-hand upright at the very last moment. For New Zealand their first defeat on Irish soil was as close as that.

Final Score: New Zealand 10, Ireland 10

Neath-Aberavon

The Gnoll, Neath, Wednesday, January 24, 1973
Attendance: 15,000

Teams and Scorers

All Blacks			*Neath-Aberavon*		
Karam	6C P T		W. Davies	Neath	
Hales			D. Jenkins	Neath	
Hurst	T		G. Ball (capt.)	Neath	
Batty	T		J. Thomas	Aberavon	
			K. Collier	Neath	
Sayers	T				
Burgess	2T				
			D. Parker	Neath	
Colling			C. Shell	Aberavon	
Whiting, G. J.			G. Shaw	Neath	
Norton			M. Howells	Aberavon	
McNicol			R. Lewis	Neath	
Macdonald			A. Martin	Aberavon	P
Haden			W. Mainwaring	Aberavon	
Stewart			D. Morris	Neath	
Wyllie			W. Lauder	Neath	
Kirkpatrick (capt.)	T		O. Alexander	Aberavon	
Sub:					
Williams for Batty					
	43 pts			3 pts	

Referee: P. E. Hughes (England)

Their biggest win in Britain, this was one of the All Blacks' great crowd-pleasing displays, to be numbered, unfortunately, on the fingers of one hand. It was a massacre and so much in control of the proceedings were the tourists that only once did they need to bother to send the ball out for a wing to score—the midfield backs could help themselves to tries.

As with their other high-scoring games, Colling and Burgess were paired behind the pack and Burgess belatedly on this tour demonstrated to the crowd just how exciting a runner with the

ball he can be. It is idle to conjecture just how much more
entertaining the tour would have been if less frequently Burgess
had been forced to stand by as Going played his 9-man rugby
and, when given the ball, pursued a kicking policy not neces-
sarily of his own choosing.

Whatever defiance there was from the Neath-Aberavon side
came in the first quarter of an hour, when a Karam penalty
(**All Blacks 3, Neath-Aberavon 0**) was replied to by one from
Martin. (**3–3**) Batty unselfishly lobbed the ball infield to Kirkpatrick when he might have scored himself, for his captain to
start the flood of tries. Karam converted. (**9–3**) That try from
a line-out was then followed by another from a set piece, when
from a scrum there were so many All Blacks lined up to score
that Karam went over with three men on hand outside him.
He converted his own try.

Half-time: All Blacks 15, Neath-Aberavon 3

Within eight minutes of the turn-around Wyllie, collecting
from a ruck, drew the last defender and presented Batty with
a try (**19–3**) and barely a minute later when from another ruck
Colling span the ball out to Burgess he speeded it on his way
by tapping it to Hurst instead of taking it and passing, a ploy
which sufficiently confused the defence for Hurst to cross the
line unopposed. Karam converted (**25–3**).

The All Blacks were getting possession at will and by now the
Neath-Aberavon tackling had progressed from weak to pitiful.
From another ruck Burgess sliced right through the opposing
line to score beside the posts. Karam converted. (**31–3**) From
a tap penalty he was given the ball at almost the same place
and then proceeded to do an almost identical repeat, Karam
again adding the extra points. (**37–3**)

Sayers then produced one of the best things he did on tour,
making ground through a group of would-be tacklers, appearing
to be hemmed in but then dodging his way through to emerge
in unoccupied territory on the Neath-Aberavon line. Karam
converted. (**43–3**)

In the final minutes the All Blacks twice were awarded
penalties right under the posts. Karam could easily have boosted
his personal points tally: the tourists could as simply raised

their highest total in Britain. But instead they continued to run the ball and I suppose it could be said for Neath-Aberavon that they did at least hold on long enough to prevent the ignominy of the half-century going up on the board.

Final Score: All Blacks 43, Neath-Aberavon 3

Barbarians

Cardiff Arms Park, Saturday, January 27, 1973
Attendance: 50,000

Teams and Scorers

All Blacks		*Barbarians*		
Karam	P	J. P. R. Williams	London Welsh	T
Williams		D. J. Duckham	Coventry	
Robertson		S. J. Dawes (capt.)	London Welsh	
Batty	2T	C. M. H. Gibson	NIFC	
		J. C. Bevan	Cardiff	T
Hurst				
Burgess				
		P. Bennett	Llanelli	2C P
Going		G. O. Edwards	Cardiff	T
Lambert		A. B. Carmichael	West of Scotland	
Urlich		J. V. Pullin	Bristol	
Whiting, G. J.		R. J. McLoughlin	Blackrock Coll	
Macdonald		R. M. Wilkinson	Cambridge U	
Whiting, P. J.		W. J. McBride	Ballymena	
Scown		J. F. Slattery	Blackrock Coll	T
Wyllie		D. L. Quinnell	Llanelli	
Kirkpatrick (capt.)		T. P. David	Llanelli	
Sub:				
Colling for Going				

11 pts   23 pts

Referee: M. G. Domercq (France)

In 1964 the Barbarians and the All Blacks had turned on a
superb game of rugby, with the Cardiff crowd screaming 'More,
more, more!' as Whineray's tourists took their score to 36–3.
Then in 1967 the injury-time 11–6 win of Lochore's men was
one of the most exciting matches ever seen at Twickenham.
It was too much to expect three great Barbarian-All Black
matches in a row . . . but that was precisely what we got.
And this one was perhaps the greatest of the three, especially

in British eyes, since it was the Baa-Baas who triumphed this time.

With only two minutes on the clock there was one of the most magnificent team tries ever seen at the Arms Park—a 100-yard affair with seven men handling—and this was just the prelude to some of the most glorious rugby even the oldest veteran could remember. The bulk of it came from the side containing twelve of the 1971 Lions but to their credit the All Blacks kept faith throughout with the open rugby tradition of the Baa-Baas, never sewing things up and playing to their forward strength to avoid the defeat that would make theirs the worst ever record for New Zealand teams in the British Isles.

Under the leadership of Lions' captain John Dawes it was such an all-round team effort that it would perhaps be unfair to start singling out such players as Duckham for his exhilarating runs from counter-attack positions. All of them, right down the list from John Williams at full-back, the Lions lived right up to their reputations. Perhaps the fairest thing to do would be to single out Tom David, who far from being a Lion had at this stage not even been capped for his country, as the best forward on the field.

Rarely has there been such a sensational opening to a major match and that first try originated from a kick infield by right-wing Bryan Williams. The ball bounced through to within ten yards of the Barbarians' line on the opposite side of the field. Bennett retrieved it and—this being a Baa-Baa match—opened up. With a series of brilliant sidesteps he eluded four All Blacks before passing to John Williams in front of the posts. Tackled around the neck, Williams managed to get the ball to Pullin, who transferred to Dawes. Starting with a beautiful dummy, Dawes moved play up to halfway, where he passed infield to David, who took things past the New Zealanders' 10-yard line before being brought down by Graham Whiting. But one-handed he managed to toss the ball out to Quinnell, who had Bevan on the touchline beside him. As Quinnell passed to the winger all seemed set for an exciting Bevan run but it was then that Gareth Edwards literally took matters into his own hands and intercepted his team-mate's pass. With the crowd screaming, Edwards triumphantly outdistanced the defenders over the remaining 30 yards to the line, for the try that will be re-shown again and again on TV for years to come. (**All Blacks 0, Barbarians 4**)

It's just a pity that we haven't the space here to go into such detail about two of the Baa-Baas' other three tries (by Bevan and John Williams), plus a near miss by Bevan and a disallowed try by Dawes, all of them in precisely the same vein. Suffice to say that it was Lions rugby at its most devastating, as though Dawes and Co. were out to show the British public what their 1971 side had been like when in top gear in New Zealand.

In the 31st minute Bennett kicked a penalty (**0–7**) which stemmed from Wyllie obstructing Edwards at the back of a ruck and two minutes later when Going was trying to cope with a bad heel from a scrum in the All Black 25 Edwards and Slattery harassed him, for the Irishman to pick up and swivel over when tackled on the line. Bennett converted. (**0—13**)

A minute before half-time Burgess knocked on, to set up a typical Lions counter-attack situation. Quinnell took the advantage allowed by French referee Domercq, who played his full part in making it such a marvellous game to watch, and when the ball went to Dawes he tossed a long pass out to Bevan, who had the crowd again in an uproar as he got the better of five converging tacklers in his journey to the line. (**0–17**)

Never in the history of New Zealand rugby had an All Black side sucked their oranges with such a deficit on the board against them.

Half-time: All Blacks 0, Barbarians 17

Based on the proceedings so far, the crowd settled down to watch what looked as though it was going to be an historic pile-up of points against the tourists. But again to their credit the All Blacks fought back. Karam started the revival with a penalty from a crooked Edwards put-in near his posts (**3–17**) and thus ensured his own niche in rugby history by being the first All Black to score in every one of his appearances in Britain. Then it was concerted pressure from the tourists that brought them two good tries.

The first, 11 minutes from the restart, came when Burgess clutched from the turf a shocking pass from Going, now very much hampered by the damaged ankle he had started with. The delay in Burgess getting the line going turned out to be a blessing, for it gave Bryan Williams time to come around from his wing and be in the attack beside Batty, whom he sent away in the clear. (7–17) Then half-way through the last quarter, with Going replaced by Colling, it was Hurst who engineered the next try, if rather fortuitously. What seemed to be a kick to the corner for Batty instead went straight out in his direction. He snapped up the ball and with only John Williams to beat, did it brilliantly. At one and the same time he kicked past Williams' right and ran to his left. The for once bewildered Williams was so outfoxed that when Batty reached the ball in goal he had time to pick it up and debate for a moment or two whether he should run nearer the posts before touching down. (11–17) He wasn't given full credit for this wonderful try by the crowd because he was in their bad books, having had, with David, one of the few punch-ups of the match.

With the All Blacks only six points behind now, the game was very much on the boil. There was a niggling feeling at the back of British minds that, as in 1967, the tourists could deny the Baa-Baas their win. But then the matter was settled by a Baa-Baa try that climaxed one of the longest sessions of sustained inter-passing between backs and forwards that I've ever seen in a major fixture.

Duckham started it when he counter-attacked from a mis-kick to touch. When his weaving run into midfield was blocked the ball was tossed around with abandon and just as everyone felt that this exciting attack had bogged down Gibson started it all over again by racing off out to the right. Again the ball went back and forth among the Baa-Baas, eventually to reach John Williams, who left Karam standing with a superb swerve. And Bennett's conversion from near touch put the lid on it.

Final Score: All Blacks 11, Barbarians 23

French Selection

Tarbes, Wednesday, January 31, 1973
Attendance: 16,000

Teams and Scorers

All Blacks		*French Selection*		
Morris	P	J.-M. Aguirre	Bagneres	P
Williams	C P	M. Lacoste	Pau	
Robertson	T	C. Pecune	Tarbes	
Skudder		P. Nadal	Mont-de-Marsan	
		A. Compaes	Lourdes	
Parkinson				
Stevens				
		A. Moretti	Marmande	
Colling		G. Pardies	Agen	
McNicol		J.-L. Asarete	St-Jean-de-Lux	
Urlich		J.-L. Ugartemendia	St-Jean-de-Lux	
Clark		A. Darriesecq	Biarritz	
Eliason		J.-P. Bastiat	Dax	
Whiting, P. J.		A. Plantefol	Agen	
Kirkpatrick (capt.)		J.-C. Skrela	Stade Toulousain	
Sutherland		B. Dauga (capt.)	Mont-de-Marsan	
Holmes		P. Peron	Racing	
	12 pts			3 pts

Referee: Capt. P. Lillington (England)

In unfriendly conditions—a muddy pitch and a biting wind—
the All Blacks took some considerable time to settle down to
asserting their dominance over what was supposed to be one of
the weaker 'selections'. In the first half they could only manage
to be up by two penalties and when this lead was cut to three
points with ten minutes to go there could have been an upset
had the locals been able to produce that extra bit of fire in the
closing stages.

They had already done extremely well, under the leadership
of veteran Benoit Dauga, most capped (50) Frenchman, who

was the inspiration of their superiority to the All Blacks in the line-out and almost an equal amount of ball from the rucks. Showing up better in the backs, a great game by scrum-half Pardies, was a reason for this and also constantly earning applause among their back division for defence and attack was full-back Aquirre, who earned himself in this match a place in France's side for the Test, only to have the cruel luck of missing his first cap through injury just a couple of days before the game.

Morris opened the score with a penalty after just two minutes (**All Blacks 3, French Selection 0**) but despite the great industry of Sutherland and Kirkpatrick, who had one of the most hard-working games of the tour, the necessary forward superiority could not be established. Next points had to come again from a kick, four minutes from the end of the half, when Bryan Williams put over a 53-yarder, one of the biggest and best he has done.

Half-time: All Blacks 6, French Selection 0

It was Williams who almost got the first try of the match when, following a kick ahead, he was just beaten to the touch in goal. But this was against the run of the play in much of this half, when the All Blacks' chief occupation seemed to be keeping the French out. Sutherland decided to be tough about it and when he roughed up Bastiat, Aquirre successfully goaled the 43-yard penalty. (**6-3**)

On the defensive, the tourists were relieved by a tremendous down-wind kick by Stevens which found touch 70 yards ahead of him. At the line-out the All Blacks caught cleanly, for their backs to confuse the Frenchmen with a dummy scissors, finished off by a good run for the line by Robertson. Williams converted.

Final Score: All Blacks 12, French Selection 3

French Selection

Municipal Stadium, Lyons, Saturday, February 3, 1973
Attendance: 17,000

Teams and Scorers

All Blacks		French Selection		
Karam	2C P	H. Cabrol	Beziers	
Hales		J. F. Philliponneau	Montferrand	T
Robertson		R. Bertranne	Toulon	T
Batty	2T	J. Maso	Narbonne	
		A. Dubertrand	Montferrand	
Hurst				
Burgess				
		J.-L. Berot (capt.)	St Toulousain	
Stevens	T	M. Pebeyre	Montferrand	
Lambert		J. Ordioni	Toulon	
Norton		A. Clerc	Racing	
Whiting, G. J.		J. L. Marton	Beziers	
Haden		B. Boffelli	Aurillac	
Whiting, P. J.		C. Spanghero	Narbonne	
Kirkpatrick (capt.)		M. Vachvilli	Brive	
Wyllie	T	R. Fite	Brive	
Stewart		E. August	Racing	
	23 pts			8 pts

Referee: A. M. Hosie (Scotland)

This convincing win didn't look as though it was going to be in the scrappy first half. But then a flash of Batty brilliance sparked off the All Blacks to apply their expertise against this strong Selection, containing 11 Internationals. The French crowd forgave Batty for that try, and his other. They'd heard so much about him and had been so looking forward to seeing him, and he didn't let them down. Also they were so much impressed by Stevens, who played such a polished game in this, his first outing of the tour at scrum-half, that they wondered what the All Blacks were worrying about as regard the possi-

bility of both Going and Colling being unavailable for the Test.
At this magnificent stadium which made visiting British
pressmen envious when they thought of provincial facilities at
home, a *mauvais introduction* by Pebeyre at a scrum enabled
Karam to goal from 40 yards when the game was merely three
minutes old. (**All Blacks 3, French Selection 0**) It seemed
that all the rest of the half was going to be indecisive until, in
the 39th minute, the French backs were on the attack and
centre Bertranne, seemingly uncertain as to whether to pass to
Cabrol, the full-back, who had come into the line, or winger
Philliponneau, wound up by causing it to drop between them.
Batty snapped it up and nobody had a chance of stopping him
getting across the 50 yards of vacant territory between him and
the posts. Karam converted.

Half-time: All Blacks 9, French Selection 0

After seven minutes Stevens succeeded in getting across on
the tight side of a ruck after first Kirkpatrick and then Karam
had each been brought down just short. (**13–0**) The home side
retaliated when Philliponneau was put across following a back
movement, although there seemed to be some question about
the validity of the try, as with the other one they were to score.
Karam appeared to put him over the dead ball line before he
grounded. (**13–4**)

The All Blacks' third try came when there was a five-yard
scrum and Stevens fed Wyllie on the blind side and his weight
took him over near the corner. (**17–4**) A brilliant movement by
Pebeyre to Maso to Bertranne saw the last named score, also in
the corner, but the All Blacks were visibly surprised that it was
allowed because it seemed clearly to have gone straight through
the tunnel of the scrum. (**17–8**)

Batty completed proceedings by getting possession from a
ruck and darting in for a try with all the explosive speed which
earned for him the nickname in France of 'Dynamite'. Karam
converted.

Final Score: All Blacks 23, French Selection 8

French Selection

Clermont-Ferrand, Wednesday, February 7, 1973
Attendance: 10,000

Teams and Scorers

All Blacks		French Selection	
Morris		M. Droitecourt	Montferrand
Williams	C	J.-P. Puidebois	Brive
Parkinson		G. Anastique	Montferrand
Skudder		C. Badin	Chalon
		J. Gourdon	PUC
Sayers			
Stevens			
		J. Roques	Brive
Going (capt.)		R. Astre (capt.)	Beziers D
Clark		J. Constantino	Montferrand
Urlich		J. Fleury	Stade Clermontois
McNicol		M. Repellin	La Voulte
Haden		I. Sappa	Nice
Macdonald		J.-C. Rossignol	Brive
Sutherland		M. Dusang	Vichy
Scown		A. Faillon	La Voulte
Holmes		J.-P. Rives	Beaumont
Subs:			
Hurst	T		
for Parkinson			
Batty for Sayers			
6 pts			3 pts

Referee: M. Johnson (England)

This was almost another midweek disaster. (The All Blacks had failed to win a quarter of their midweek fixtures.) Against a team of 'unknowns', none of them being current Internationals, the tourists found themselves yet again in the position of playing out the final stages with their opponents only needing to snatch an opportunist try—like the inferior boxer's lucky punch—for victory. In fact right at the end they muffed a relatively easy penalty that would have made it a draw.

Going played mainly to test out his damaged ankle and although it stood up to the trial he had an unhappy afternoon otherwise. Time and again his breaks were foiled, caught either by his opposite number, Astre, or the quick off the mark flankers Dusang and Rives. The other back-row man, Faillon was just as lively and he, in combination with locks Sappa and Rossignol, dominated the line-out. Roques, no kicking fly-half he, used possession such as this to great advantage and sent his outsides off on some exciting runs.

It proved lucky for the All Blacks that Parkinson and Sayers had to go off. Replaced by Hurst and Batty it meant a re-juggling of the backline, with Williams going into the centre. The changes brought an improvement in the tackling and it was this that was to keep out the free-running French backs, notably the youthful winger Gourdon, who threatened to score every time the ball came to him.

In perfect conditions the only score in the first half came when full-back Droitecourt had an unfortunate lapse. He failed to field a centering kick from Williams. Haden was up there to get possession and a long pass out to Hurst saw him go over by the posts, for Karam to do the simple conversion. (**All Blacks 6, French Selection 0**) For those interested in collecting odd statistics, this was the only score by any of the 16 substitutes used on the tour.

Half-time: All Blacks 6, French Selection 0

Drop kicks from a fly-half are common, from a scrum-half rare. But in the ninth minute Astre showed how it can be done. It was executed so quickly that nobody seemed to quite know what he was up to. Getting the ball from a heel he moved out to the side of the scrum and sent over a high, clean drop from 40 yards. (**6–3**)

It was only that resolute tackling, especially by Williams, that stopped the French from adding a try and it was Droitecourt who was the unfortunate one again when four minutes from the close he missed the vital penalty from 27 yards.

Final Score: All Blacks 6, French Selection 3

While Murdoch wonders and Gareth Edwards starts to celebrate, Referee Johnny Johnson has no hesitation in signalling a penalty against John Williams for rabbiting, rather than a try that would have changed Wales's 16-19 defeat to victory.

TWO DISALLOWED TRIES
THAT WOULD HAVE MADE ALL THE DIFFERENCE

Batty fails to stop Preece, supported by Morley, from going over in the England match. A try at this stage would have put them back in the game and could well have staved off their 0-9 defeat. But Warfield's pass to Preece was ruled forward.

"THE MATCH OF A LIFETIME"

That's what the BBC called the Barbarians' 23-12 triumph over the All Blacks when, after the tour was over, they brought it back for another TV showing 'by public demand'.

(*Opposite, top*) Three who played an important part in making it the great spectacle it was. Gareth Edwards, who scored the sensational opening try; French Referee Domercq, who kept everything flowing beautifully; Kirkpatrick, who insisted his team spin the ball in Baa-Baa style, even when defeat was inevitable. (*Opposite, below*) Duckham beats Hurst in the course of one of his numerous scintillating runs. (*Right*) Bevan eludes Bryan Williams (plus others) on the way to his great try. (*Below*) The Slattery try: Going (on ground) has been robbed by Gareth Edwards, Slattery picks up and despite Burgess grabbing his wrist and Karam on the line manages to power his way over.

TRIUMPH: Fran Cotton, captain of North West Counties, is chaired off the field by Lansbury and Wardlow after their 16-14 win over the All Blacks.

THE TWO SIDES OF THE COIN AT WORKINGTON

DEJECTION: Ian Eliason reflects what it feels like to be a member of the first New Zealand team ever to be beaten by an English provincial side.

MATCH NO. 30

France

Parc des Princes, Paris, Saturday, February 10, 1973
Attendance: 55,000

Teams and Scorers

New Zealand		*France*		
Karam	2P	J. Cantoni	Beziers	
Williams		R. Bertranne	Toulon	T
Robertson		C. Dourthe	Dax	T
Batty		J. P. Lux	Dax	
		A. Compaes	Lourdes	
Hurst				
Burgess				
		J. P. Romeu	Montferrand	C P
Going		M. Barrau	Toulousain	
Lambert		J. Iracabal	Bayonne	
Norton		R. Benesis	Agen	
Whiting, G. J.		J. L. Asareto	St-Jean-de-Lux	
Whiting, P. J.		E. Cester	Valence	
Macdonald		A. Esteve	Beziers	
Wyllie		O. Saisset	Beziers	
Sutherland		W. Spanghero (capt.)	Narbonne	
Kirkpatrick (capt.)		P. Biemouret	Agen	

Sub :
M. Droitecourt (Montferrand) for Cantoni

6 pts 13 pts

Referee: D. P. D'Arcy (Ireland)

In the last match of their 1935 tour the All Blacks had been trounced 13–0 by England and on this day there was the same end-of-tour look of a stale, listless side completely dominated by their opponents. Only through their wasteful attitude to the many chances they made for themselves did France not make their scoreline as convincing as England had in those far-off pre-war days.

Keynote of the French victory was that the New Zealand back row of Kirkpatrick, Sutherland and Wyllie in combination with Going were thoroughly overshadowed and outplayed by the Spanghero-Saisset-Biemouret trio in concert with Max Barrau. Time and again they swarmed over the field and what the French call 'the Black Tide' never seemed to be able to do the same thing. The New Zealanders were never allowed to exert their accustomed superiority in the rucks.

Sensing the trouble they would be likely to have in their other usual springboard for All Black attacks—the line-out—France plumped for the shortened version. Although not always successful in this, over-eagerness to get going often resulting in misfielding of the throw-in, they at least held the New Zealand forwards in check in this sphere.

Subdued at the rucks and in the line-out, New Zealand had no answer to the liveliness of the French backs. No fewer than four times in the first twenty minutes France should have scored from back movements, only to throw away 'certain' tries. Most flagrant of these was in the seventh minute when man-of-the-match Spanghero, breaking from a ruck, sent out a pass which gave Dourthe, Lux and Compaes a three-to-one situation against Karam. It seemed unbelievable that Lux should omit to give Compaes the scoring pass.

Such squandering of opportunities could not go on indefinitely. In the 25th minute, when one of their shortened line-outs worked properly, the ebullient Barrau darted off into midfield and Dourthe ran in powerfully from 20 yards. Ironically, however, even this could have been added to the muffed chances since Referee D'Arcy might well have whistled up Barrau for a forward pass. (**New Zealand 0, France 4**)

Almost at once Karam replied with a 35-yard penalty (**3–4**) but just before the end of this half France scored again from the best movement of the match. At a scrum in midfield at just about halfway Spanghero picked up and sent Barrau scurrying off. He was up with him to take a reverse pass, with the All Blacks, dropping back, looking all at sea, and as he went down to a tackle he shot the ball out to the supporting backs. Dourthe took play up into the 25 before transferring to Bertranne on the right wing, for him to sail over with four defenders vainly snapping at his heels. Romeu converted.

Half-time: New Zealand 3, France 10

Not as open and as exciting to watch as the first half, the second session produced only two scores from kicks. When Biemouret broke too early from a scrum Karam goaled an easy one from in front of the posts **(6–10)** in the 48th minute and ten minutes later Lambert was not ten yards back at a shortened line-out and Romeu was successful with his shot at goal. **(6–13)**

With the match not over by any means the All Blacks seemed quite incapable of producing the sort of fire needed to retrieve the situation. Going kicked and when he did send out to Burgess, he kicked too with the same aimless sense of desperation. And as the game drew to a close it was all French pressure against a clearly jaded side.

Final Score: New Zealand 6, France 13

PART THREE

Facts and Figures

	Province	Occupation	Age	Height	Weight
Full-backs					
Morris, T. J. (Trevor)	Nelson Bays	Teacher	30	5.10½	12.7
Karam, J. F. (Joe)	Wellington	Sales rep	20	5.8	12.4
Wings					
Williams, B. G. (Bryan)	Auckland	Law student	21	5.10	13.8
Hales, D. A. (Duncan)	Canterbury	Student	24	5.10	13.0
Batty, G. B. (Grant)	Wellington	Insurance clerk	20	5.5½	10.7
Skudder, G. R. (George)	Waikato	Teacher	24	5.11	13.0
Centres					
Robertson, B. (Bruce)	Counties	Trainee teacher	20	6.0½	13.0
Hurst, I. A. (Ian)	Canterbury	Student	21	5.11	13.4
Five-eighths					
Parkinson, R. M. (Mike)	Poverty Bay	Freezing worker	24	5.11	13.0
Sayers, M. (Mark)	Wellington	Teacher	25	5.11	12.12
Burgess, R. E. (Bob)	Manawatu	Student	23	5.10	11.12
Stevens, I. N. (Ian)	Wellington	Clerk	24	5.10	11.7
Half-backs					
Going, S. M. (Sid) Vice-Captain	North Auckland	Farmer	29	5.7½	11.7
Colling, G. L. (Lindsay)	Otago	Clerk	26	5.9	11.10
No. 8s					
Sutherland, A. R. (Alan)	Marlborough	Sales rep	28	6.3	16.8
Holmes, B. (Bevan)	North Auckland	Teacher	26	6.2	15.4
Flankers					
Kirkpatrick, I. A. (Ian) Captain	Poverty Bay	Farmer	26	6.2½	16.0
Scown, A. I. (Alistair)	Taranaki	Farmer	26	6.1	15.0
Stewart, K. W. (Ken)	Southland	Farmer	19	6.1	14.12
Wyllie, A. J. (Alex)	Canterbury	Farmer	27	6.1	16.0
Locks					
Eliason, I. M. (Ian)	Taranaki	Farmer	27	6.4	15.10
Haden, A. (Andy)	Auckland	Student	22	6.5	17.4
Macdonald, H. H. (Hamish)	Canterbury	Farmer	26	6.3	15.12
Whiting, P. J. (Peter)	Auckland	Teacher	25	6.4½	17.4
Props					
Whiting, G. J. (Graham)	King Country	Insurance salesman	26	6.3½	17.6
*Matheson, J. (Jeff)	Otago	Farmer	24	5.11½	15.10
†Murdoch, K. (Keith)	Otago	Ballet dancer	29	6.0	17.0
Lambert, K. K. (Kent)	Manawatu	Student	20	5.10	15.5

	Province	Occupation	Age	Height	Weight
Hookers					
Norton, R. W. (Tane)	Canterbury	Bank officer	29	5.11	13.12
Urlich, R. A. (Ron)	Auckland	Draughtsman	28	6.1	14.4

Average age of team: 24 Forwards' weight: 15 st 11 lb Height: 6 ft 1 in.

Manager: E. L. (Ernie) Todd Assistant Manager/Coach: R. M. (Bob) Duff

	Province	Occupation	Age	Height	Weight
Replacements					
†Clark, L. A. (Lindsay)	Otago	Farmer	27	6.0	16.7
*McNicol, S. M. (Sandy)	Wanganui	Farmer	27	6.2	16.12

WHO DID THE SCORING

		In Britain and France					Test Appearances	
	Matches	T	P	C	D	Pts	Tour	Career
Morris	10		12	5	2	52	—	3
Karam	19	2	24	29		138	WSEIF	5
Williams	22(1)	7	4	2	1	15	WSEIF	15
Hales	16	5				20	WS	5
Batty	21(2)	19				76	WSEIF	5
Skudder	12(2)	3				12	—	1
Robertson	14	3				12	SEIF	6
Hurst	15(1)	7				28	IF	2
Parkinson	13	4				16	WSE	6
Sayers	14(1)	4				16	—	—
Burgess	18	5				20	W IF	7
Stevens	13	3				12	SE	2
Going	18(1)	3		3	1	21	WSEIF	19
Colling	14(1)	2				8	—	—
Sutherland	17	5				20	W EIF	10
Holmes	11						—	—
Kirkpatrick	23	5				20	WSEIF	24
Scown	13(3)	1				4	WS	3
Stewart	11	1				4	—	—
Wyllie	18	5				20	WSEIF	10
Eliason	10						—	—
Haden	15	2				8	—	—
Macdonald	16						WSEIF	5
Whiting, P. J.	20(1)	1				4	WSEIF	11
Whiting, G. J.	19(1)						SEIF	6
Matheson	9						WS	5
Murdoch	8	1				4	W	3
Lambert	15(1)			1		2	SEIF	4
Norton	14						WSEIF	12
Urlich	16	1				4	—	2
Clark	7(1)						—	—
McNicol	5						—	—
		89	40	40	4	568		

Note: Figures in brackets indicate how many of total appearances were as substitute. Lambert was a substitute against Scotland, Scown against Wales.

DETAILS OF THE MATCHES

Match No.	Date	Opponents	Venue	Result		Half-time	
1	Oct 28	Western Counties	Gloucester	W 39	12	21	0
2	Oct 31	Llanelli	Llanelli	L 3	9	3	6
3	Nov 4	Cardiff	Cardiff	W 20	4	10	0
4	Nov 8	Cambridge U	Cambridge	W 34	3	8	0
5	Nov 11	London Counties	Twickenham	W 24	3	12	3
6	Nov 15	Leinster	Dublin	W 17	9	3	0
7	Nov 18	Ulster	Belfast	W 19	6	9	0
8	Nov 22	N W Counties	Workington	L 14	16	10	9
9	Nov 26	Scottish Districts	Hawick	W 26	6	10	6
10	Nov 28	Gwent	Ebbw Vale	W 16	7	6	0
11	**Dec 2**	**Wales**	**Cardiff**	**W 19**	**16**	**13**	**3**
12	Dec 6	Midland Counties W	Moseley	L 8	16	4	16
13	Dec 9	N E Counties	Bradford	W 9	3	6	3
14	Dec 12	Edinburgh & Glasgow	Glasgow	W 16	10	3	4
15	**Dec 16**	**Scotland**	**Murrayfield**	**W 14**	**9**	**6**	**0**
16	Dec 20	Southern Counties	Oxford	W 23	6	11	0
17	Dec 26	Combined Services	Twickenham	W 31	10	13	0
18	Dec 30	East Glamorgan	Cardiff	W 20	9	10	9
19	Jan 2	S W Counties	Redruth	W 30	7	4	3
20	**Jan 6**	**England**	**Twickenham**	**W 9**	**0**	**6**	**0**
21	Jan 10	Newport	Newport	W 20	15	6	6
22	Jan 13	E Midland Counties	Leicester	W 43	12	18	6
23	Jan 16	Munster	Cork	D 3	3	0	0
24	**Jan 20**	**Ireland**	**Dublin**	**D 10**	**10**	**6**	**3**
25	Jan 24	Neath & Aberavon	Neath	W 43	3	15	3
26	Jan 27	Barbarians	Cardiff	L 11	23	0	17
27	Jan 31	French Selection	Tarbes	W 12	3	6	0
28	Feb 3	French Selection	Lyons	W 23	8	9	0
29	Feb 7	French Selection	Clermont-Ferrand	W 6	3	6	0
30	**Feb 10**	**France**	**Paris**	**L 6**	**13**	**3**	**10**

SCORERS FOR AND AGAINST

Match No.	All Blacks	Opponents
1	Karam P 4C, Williams 3T, Robertson T, Parkinson 2T, Colling T	P. E. Butler 2P C, M. Burton T
2	Karam P	E. T. E. Bergiers T, A. Hill P, P. Bennett C
3	Karam 2P C, Batty T, Sayers T, Kirkpatrick T	G. Edwards T
4	Karam C, Batty 4T, Going 2C, Sutherland 2T, Wyllie T	J. M. Howard P
5	Karam 2C T, Williams T, Batty T, Hurst T, Sutherland T	A. M. Jorden P
6	Williams P, Skudder T, Going C, Wyllie T, P. J. Whiting T	A. H. Ensor P C, W. Duggan T
7	Karam 3P C, Hales T, Burgess T	B. D. E. Marshall C, H. W. Steele T
8	Morris 2P, Batty T, Skudder T	C. S. Wardlow D, P. S. Maxwell 2T A. R. Cowman P C
9	Karam 2P 2C, Hales T, Skudder T, Parkinson T, Going T	P. C. Brown 2P
10	Morris P C D, Stevens T, Haden T	R. Pugh P, G. Turner T
11	Karam 5P, Murdoch T	J. C. Bevan T, P. Bennett 4P
12	Hurst T, Sayers T	S. J. Doble P C, D. J. Duckham T, M. J. Cooper T, J. F. Finlan D
13	Karam C, Batty T, Going D	A. G. B. Old P
14	Karam 2P C, Sutherland T, Urlich T	F. N. F. Dall T, D. W. Morgan 2P
15	Karam C, Batty T, Going T, Wyllie T	A. R. Irvine 2P, I. R. McGeechan D
16	Morris P 2C, Williams 2T, Hales T, Haden T	P. Cadle T, D. Llewelyn C
17	Morris 4P 2C D, Batty T, Parkinson T, Scown T	P. M. Davies T, P. J. Larter 2P
18	Karam 2P C, Hales 2T, Stevens T	C. Bolderson P, I. Hopkins P, R. Evans D
19	Batty 3T, Hurst 2T, Burgess T, Lambert C, Kirkpatrick T	K. C. Plummer T, A. P. Pearn P
20	Karam C, Williams D, Kirkpatrick T	—
21	Morris 2P, Williams 2P T, Sayers T	R. Williams 2P C D, J. Williams T
22	Karam P 4C, Robertson T, Batty T, Hurst T, Burgess T, Colling T, Stewart T, Sutherland T, Kirkpatrick T	D. F. Whibley 2P C, J. A. Allen T
23	Morris P	B. J. McGann P
24	Karam C, Going T, Wyllie T	T. O. Grace T, B. J. McGann 2P

147

SCORERS FOR AND AGAINST—*continued*

Match No.	*All Blacks*	*Opponents*
25	Karam P 6C T, Hurst T, Batty T, Sayers T, Burgess 2T, Kirkpatrick T	A. Martin P
26	Karam P, Batty 2T	J. P. R. Williams T, J. C. Bevan T, P. Bennett P 2C, G. O. Edwards T, J. F. Slattery T
27	Morris P, Williams P C, Robertson T	J.-M. Aguirre P
28	Karam P 2C, Batty 2T, Stevens T, Wyllie T	J. F. Philliponneau T, R. Bertranne T
29	Williams C, Hurst T	P. Astre P
30	Karam 2P	C. Dourthe T, R. Bertranne T, J.-P. Romeu P C

NEW ZEALAND TOURS TO BRITAIN, FRANCE AND AMERICA

1905–6

	P	W	D	L	F	A	Internationals		
In Britain	32	31	–	1	830	39	v Scotland W 12 7	v Ireland W 15 0	
France	1	1	–	–	38	8	England W 15 0	Wales L 0 3	
America	2	2	–	–	108	12	France W 38 8		
Full Tour	35	34	–	1	976	59			

1924–5

	P	W	D	L	F	A			
In Britain	28	28	–	–	654	98	v England W 17 11	v Ireland W 6 0	
France	2	2	–	–	67	14	France W 30 6	Wales W 19 0	
Canada	2	2	–	–	117	4			
	32	32	–	–	838	116			

1935–6

	P	W	D	L	F	A			
In Britain	28	24	1	3	431	180	v Scotland W 18 8	v Ireland W 17 9	
Canada	2	2	–	–	59	3	England L 0 13	Wales L 12 13	
	30	26	1	3	490	183			

1953–4

	P	W	D	L	F	A			
In Britain	28	24	2	2	417	102	v Scotland W 3 0	v Ireland W 14 3	
France	2	–	–	2	8	14	England W 5 0	Wales L 8 13	
America	5	5	–	–	152	23	France L 0 3		
	35	29	2	4	577	139			

1963–4

	P	W	D	L	F	A			
In Britain	30	28	1	1	508	137	v Scotland D 0 0	v Ireland W 6 5	
France	4	4	–	–	60	16	England W 14 0	Wales W 6 0	
Canada	2	2	–	–	45	6	France W 12 3		
	36	34	1	1	613	159			

1967–8

	P	W	D	L	F	A			
In Britain	11	10	1	–	207	78	v England W 23 11	v Wales W 13 6	
France	4	4	–	–	87	51	France W 21 15	Scotland W 14 3	
Canada	2	2	–	–	76	6			
	17	16	1	–	370	135			

1972–3

	P	W	D	L	F	A			
In Britain	26	21	2	4	521	227	v Wales W 19 16	v Scotland W 14 9	
France	4	3	–	1	47	27	England W 9 0	Ireland D 10 10	
America	2	2	–	–	72	16	France L 6 13		
	32	27	2	5	640	270			